Family Child Ca

Legal and Insurance Guide

How to Reduce the Risks of Running Your Business

Early Childcare Professional Resources
Available at Front Desk

provided by

ChildCare Aware® OF KANSAS

Kansas Department for Children and Families

Louisburg Library
Bringing People and Information Together

Becoming a Family Child Care Professional

Family child care is a special profession for those who love young children. As a professional family child care provider, you must balance the skills required to care for children with those required to operate your business. Here are some tips to help you do this:

- Learn the child care regulations for your area, and follow them.
- Join your local family child care association.
- Sign up with your local child care resource and referral agency.
- Join the Child and Adult Care Food Program (CACFP).
- Find good professional advisors (such as a tax preparer, insurance agent, lawyer).
- Actively participate in training to acquire and improve your professional skills.

Additional Resources

Redleaf Press and Redleaf National Institute are two leading national organizations that share the goal of helping your family child care business succeed. Redleaf National Institute (www.redleafinstitute.org) can answer your business questions; its Web site is filled with free handouts, articles, and newsletters. Redleaf Press (www.redleafpress.org; 800-423-8309) publishes resources for family child care. We offer the following publications to support your business. (For more information, see www.redleafpress.org.)

- Starting a family child care business:
  Getting Started in the Business of Family Child Care

- Promoting your business:
  Family Child Care Marketing Guide: How to Build Enrollment and Promote Your Business as a Child Care Professional

- Creating contracts and policies:
  Family Child Care Contracts and Policies: How to Be Businesslike in a Caring Profession, 3rd Edition
  Sharing in the Caring: Family Child Care Agreement Packet for Parents and Providers

- Keeping accurate records and filing your taxes:
  Family Child Care Record-Keeping Guide, 7th Edition
  Redleaf Calendar-Keeper: A Record-Keeping System for Child Care Providers
  Family Child Care Tax Workbook and Organizer: All IRS Forms Included for Filing Your Tax Return
  Family Child Care Tax Companion: Help Your Tax Preparer Make Your Return Error-Free

- Reducing business risks:
  Family Child Care Legal and Insurance Guide: How to Reduce the Risks of Running Your Business

- Managing your money and planning for retirement:
  Download articles from www.redleafinstitute.org.

Family Child Care

Legal and Insurance Guide

How to Reduce the Risks of Running Your Business

Tom Copeland, JD,
and Mari Millard

Redleaf Press
www.redleafpress.org
800-423-8309

Published by Redleaf Press
10 Yorkton Court
St. Paul, MN 55117
www.redleafpress.org

Interior typeset in Times
Printed in the United States of America
15 14 13 12 11 10 09 08   6 7 8 9 10 11 12 13

Library of Congress Cataloging-in-Publication Data
Copeland, Tom.
  Family child care legal and insurance guide : how to reduce the risks
of running your business / by Tom Copeland and Mari Millard.
      p. cm.
  Includes index.
  ISBN 978-1-929610-45-7
  1. Child care services—United States. 2. Child care services—
Law and legislation—United States. 3. Insurance, Liability—
United States. I. Millard, Mari. II. Title.
  HQ778.63.C655 2004
  362.71'2'0973—dc22

                                     2004001066

Printed on acid-free paper

Contents

Part II: Insuring Your Business and Yourself Against Risks

Part III: Handling Legal Issues

Part IV: Choosing a Business Structure

About the Authors

Tom Copeland

Tom Copeland is the Director of Redleaf National Institute. He is a licensed attorney and has provided business assistance to family child care providers, tax preparers, and trainers since 1982. In 2003 he was presented with the Friends of NAFCC award at the annual conference of the National Association for Family Child Care. In 1998 he won the Child Care Advocate of the Year award from the Minnesota Licensed Family Child Care Association. Tom is also the author of the *Family Child Care Record-Keeping Guide, Family Child Care Tax Workbook and Organizer, Family Child Care Contracts and Policies, Family Child Care Marketing Guide, Family Child Care Inventory-Keeper,* and the *Family Child Care Audit Manual.*

Mari Millard

Mari Millard is a former associate director of Redleaf National Institute. She has a background in financial planning and has trained and advised hundreds of child care providers over the years. Prior to becoming a financial advisor, Mari supervised an extended-day program at an elementary school and was involved with her mother's family child care. Mari is currently working on an MBA at the University of St. Thomas. In her spare time, she performs with a local improvisational comedy troupe.

We Would Like Your Feedback

We would appreciate hearing your feedback about this book. Please contact us with any questions or suggestions for topics to add in future editions of this book. You can reach us at rni@redleafinstitute.org. We will post any changes or corrections to the information in this book on our Web site, www.redleafinstitute.org.

Acknowledgments

The authors would like to thank the following reviewers, who read early drafts of this book and gave us valuable feedback; we made many changes based on their suggestions. (The reviewers are not endorsing the contents of this book; only the authors are responsible for any errors.)

Insurance professionals
Liz Downs, New England Insurance Services, Inc.; Pete Freisinger, Freisinger Insurance Group; Debe Marofsky, Affiliated Insurance, Inc.; Gwen McFadden-Vincent, Risk Management Services; Don Morgan, Morgan and Associates, Inc.; Joe Silverman, DC Insurance Services, Inc.

Tax professionals
Valorie Anderson, EA, Anderson Tax Service, LLC; Pam Birkholz, EA, Pam Birkholz Tax and Accounting; Brent Gallagher, Gallagher Management Services, Inc.; Celia L. Griffin, CPA; Ed Hara, CPA, Abacus Tax; Clair Hemenway, Hemenway Accounting and Tax Service; Shelley R. Johnson, CPA, Allman & Company; Gwen Kline, VP Tax Service; Virginia Lippig, Lombard Financial Services; Julie McGrath, EA, Lelm and Associates; Catherine Nazarene, CPA, The Catherine Ditman Group; Sandy Overton, Haire's Income Tax Service; Sharon Riley, Nelson & Riley; Patsy Schmidt, A+ Bookkeeping & Tax Service; Sandy Schroeder, EA, CFP, Schroeder Financial Services; Allen Stucky, CPA, H&R Block; Robert G. Thelen, EA, Parks Tax Service, Inc.

Attorneys
Abby J. Cohen, JD, Child Care Law and Policy Consultant; Bill Jonason, JD, Dorsey and Whitney; Phyllis Karasov, JD, Moore, Costello, and Hart; Ava Yajima, JD, Child Care Law Center.

Child care resource and referral workers
Penny Chase, Community Coordinated Child Care, Madison, Wisconsin; Maria D. Fernandez, Child Care Resource and Referral, Orem, Utah; Sue Molstad, Resources for Child Caring, St. Paul, Minnesota.

Family child care providers
Dawn Abel, Michelle Anderson, Pam Arechigo, Chris Barzzett, Judy Baugus, Kay Billings, Laura Butler, Teresa A. Cole, Lynnette DiPietro, Barbie Gallini, Kay Gillock, Wendy Hahn, Lori Hameister, Colleen Mowrer, Sandra Murphy, Jane Pope, Heather Stewart, Tamera Wagner.

Other
Peter Braun, Ramsey County family child care licensor, St. Paul; Bruce Copeland; Jennifer Crandall, Colorado Enterprise Fund, Denver; Kay Hollestelle, The Children's Foundation, Washington, DC; Vicki Lipscomb, Child Nutrition Program, Inc., Charlotte, North Carolina; Kate Manolakos; Brandee Quinn, trainer, Family Service Building Tomorrow.

Thanks also to Jim Cihlar and Kathy Kolb for their project management, Jennifer Shepard for copy editing, Jesse Singer for typesetting, and Rose Brandt for editing and layout.

Introduction

The business of caring for children can be risky and expensive. Although you can never eliminate all of the risks that come with your business, you can significantly reduce them and use insurance to protect yourself against the remaining risks.

This book will explain the strategies that you can use to reduce your business risks by working closely with your licensor and the parents of the children in your care and purchasing adequate insurance to manage the remaining risks to you and your family. It will explain the key features that you should look for in business liability insurance, business property insurance, car insurance, homeowners insurance, workers' compensation insurance, umbrella liability insurance, health insurance, disability income insurance, life insurance, and long-term care insurance.

Although family child care providers regularly make decisions that can have significant legal and financial consequences, most don't have adequate insurance, and few ever consult an attorney. This book will educate you about the significant legal and insurance issues that you face every day in running your business, and explain how to

- Minimize the risks that you face in operating your business
- Defend yourself against allegations of child abuse
- Handle custody disputes between parents
- Protect the confidentiality and privacy of your clients
- Comply with the Americans with Disabilities Act
- Avoid violating the price fixing laws
- Overcome zoning and deed barriers to your business
- Find legal services at a reasonable cost
- Select the best structure for your business

Many family child care providers consider legal and insurance matters to be worrisome, intimidating, or simply boring. We understand that these are not your favorite topics. We wrote this book to offer you practical information about how to reduce your business risks and protect yourself, your family, and your business. Despite the fear and anxiety that often accompany the topics covered in this book, we believe that you will benefit greatly by spending some time learning how to manage your risks. We hope that we have written this book in a way that is easy to understand and that you will find it helpful.

If you have any questions about the issues raised in this book, you can send an e-mail to rni@redleafinstitute.org. For more information, updates, and any corrections or additions to this book, see the Business Library at www.redleafinstitute.org.

Disclaimer

This publication discusses general legal, insurance, and tax issues and is designed to provide accurate and authoritative information on those topics. It is made available with the understanding that neither the authors nor the publisher are engaged in rendering legal, insurance, tax, or other professional advice. If you require legal, insurance, or tax assistance, you should engage the services of a competent professional. Your insurance coverage is based on your insurance contracts, and you should discuss your specific insurance needs with your insurance agent.

Many of the rules and regulations discussed in this book are based on state laws, which vary greatly from state to state. Before taking any action you may want to consult an attorney or tax professional to learn about the specific laws in your state. Also, as with any publication, be sure to check whether the information in this book is still current.

PART I

Managing Your Business Risks

CHAPTER ONE

Understanding Your Business Risks

Chapter Summary
This chapter will discuss the risks that you incur by operating a family child care business and explain the five general strategies for managing risk.

Family child care is a caring profession in which children are loved, nurtured, and helped to grow. However, when you open your home to care for children, you also open yourself to a vast array of risks that are associated with operating a business, as shown in the following real-life examples:

- An eighteen-month-old was scratched while petting her child care provider's cat, and the provider was required to pay her medical bills, which totaled over $5,000.
- A provider in Minnesota lost the entire contents of her home in a tornado, but received only $2,000 from her homeowners insurance policy because of the policy limits on her business property.
- A provider in Connecticut was ordered to pay $800,000 to the parents of a child who died in her home on the second day of care due to Sudden Infant Death Syndrome.

Fortunately, there are ways to manage your business risks to avoid worst-case scenarios such as these. The first three parts of this book will provide the practical information that you need to reduce your risks and protect yourself, your family, and your business. The first step is understanding the types of risks that you face every day as a family child care provider. They include the following:

- **Injuries to children.** A child in your care falls from a slide in your backyard and breaks her arm. A toddler loses a finger after catching it in your sliding-glass door.
- **Damage to property.** A young child accidentally starts a fire in your home, resulting in damage to your living room and playroom furniture.
- **Lawsuits.** A parent sues you for a dog bite, child abuse, an injury to a child, or for administering medication that a child is allergic to.

- **Car accidents.** You are in a car accident that injures the other driver, you, your own child, and two of the children in your care, and severely damages both cars.

As a family child care provider, you are responsible for the safety of the children in your care, and since you are charging for your services, you are a professional. As a professional, you will always be held to a higher standard than a child's parent. For example, if a child dies of Sudden Infant Death Syndrome (SIDS; see page 57) in her own home, it's highly unlikely that the child's parents would be sued or charged with a crime. However, parents have successfully sued family child care providers for SIDS deaths.

In the case where the court awarded the parents $800,000, the judge said that the family child care provider had a higher "duty of care" to do everything in her power to prevent SIDS deaths. This provider had taken SIDS prevention training and had been instructed by the parent not to let the child sleep on her stomach. Nevertheless, she had failed to take action when she saw the child sleeping on her stomach. Being held accountable for your actions is the price that you pay for being a professional.

Five Strategies for Managing Your Risks

Although you will face business risks on a regular basis, there are ways to minimize your exposure to them. Here are five basic strategies that you can use to manage the risks that you incur in doing business:

- Avoid the risk
- Don't take on additional risks
- Retain the risk
- Transfer the risk
- Reduce the risk

Strategy 1: Avoid the Risk

It's possible to avoid some risks outright. For example, to avoid the potential dangers of car travel, such as a car accident (whether caused by bad weather, a drunk driver, mechanical failure, or carelessness) you could decide not to transport children in your vehicle. You could use a transportation service or keep the children close to home.

However, some risks are hard to avoid because the children enjoy them. These risks include those that you incur by having a dog, an in-ground swimming pool, a trampoline, or other playground equipment. Dog bites, in particular, are a leading cause of injuries to children in family child care. Just because your friendly golden retriever has never bit anyone yet doesn't mean that he never will. In one case a dog bit a child through the upper eyelid and cheek, causing potentially permanent eye damage and a fear of dogs that required long-term counseling.

The only sure-fire way to eliminate the serious risks that are associated with these issues is to remove the source of the risk from your program.

Strategy 2: Don't Take on Additional Risks

Be careful how you present yourself to parents. If you are an expert in a particular area, don't claim that to parents unless you are willing to use your skills and take on the responsibility that comes with doing so.

For example, one family child care provider was a nurse for many years before starting her child care business. She was proud of her nursing experience and shared it with the parents. The problem was that she was no longer a licensed nurse and hadn't had any experience or continuing education in over five years. However, the parents assumed that she would be able to diagnose illnesses and treat injuries. One morning, a mother called in a rage because she had discovered that her child had pinkeye. The mother believed that the child care provider should have noticed the child's condition immediately and informed her. She also commented that a nurse should have been able to prevent this from happening in her house.

In this case, the child care provider should have communicated to the parents the limitations of her abilities, including the facts that she was not qualified to diagnose medical conditions and that she was not continuing to refresh her nursing skills.

Another way of taking on additional risks is to include inaccurate or outdated information in your parent agreements and contracts. Only list the policies that you actually follow. If you say that you'll do something on a regular basis, do it. If you take only occasional field trips, don't say in your contract that you will do them weekly. Conduct an annual review (at least) of your policies, and if you find that you aren't following all of them, either change your ways or eliminate the policy.

It isn't necessary for your contracts to include 39 pages that detail everything that you do and how you will do it. You can keep your written policies short and inform the parents through conversations or brief notes that describe your activities and what the children are doing. However, be prepared to enforce all your rules on a consistent basis, especially those that involve the health and safety of children, such as your sickness policy. Parents may be unhappy if they find out that you aren't following your own rules, and this could lead them to leave your program or even to sue you.

Strategy 3: Retain the Risk

Retaining a risk means that you acknowledge the risk and plan on paying any costs that you might incur for that risk out of your own pocket. For example, in most cases it doesn't make sense to buy short-term disability income insurance. If you were injured and unable to work for three or four months, you would probably be able to make ends meet with your savings and help from your friends and relatives. Insurance for this type of risk is expensive and probably not worth the cost.

When you buy insurance, you can keep your insurance costs low by retaining the risk for small claims through a high deductible. However, it doesn't make sense to retain the risk for major issues, such as your long-term health, your house, the risks involved in driving a car, or the risks of being sued by a client. To cover the major financial consequences of these kinds of risks, you would have to save hundreds of thousands of dollars, at least.

Strategy 4: Transfer the Risk

If you can't avoid or retain a risk, you may be able to transfer its cost by buying insurance for that risk. This is a good strategy for covering risks that have the potential to be financially devastating. For example, if your house burned down, you probably wouldn't be able to afford to rebuild it and replace the contents. That's why people buy homeowners insurance—and the same principle applies to car insurance, health insurance, and liability insurance.

Part II of this book will provide a more detailed discussion of insurance. However, in general it doesn't make sense to buy insurance for potential losses that you could afford to cover on your own. In most cases, you only need insurance coverage for potential losses that would have a significant financial impact.

Strategy 5: Reduce the Risk

If you can't avoid a risk, it doesn't make sense to retain it, and you can't transfer all of your potential liability, then the best strategy is to look for ways to reduce its likelihood or impact. For example, let's say that you decide to transport children in your car. You buy the appropriate insurance—but you also follow a transportation risk reduction strategy. You make sure that the children are always properly buckled into their seat belts or car seats. You conduct regular safety and maintenance checks on your vehicle. Whenever possible, you drive routes that have less traffic.

You can use a combination of the above five methods to manage or minimize most of the risks that you face as a family child care provider. For example, if you decide to let the children in your care use your in-ground swimming pool, you could minimize your risk by:

- Limiting its use
- Requiring another adult to be present whenever the children use the pool
- Hiring a professional instructor to give the children swimming lessons
- Making sure that the pool is securely fenced when it's not in use
- Buying insurance to protect yourself against a potential lawsuit

The more you can incorporate these five risk management methods into your daily practices, the more you'll be able to reduce your risks of running a family child care business. In the next chapter, we'll explain how to set up your business on a professional basis to minimize your business risks. In chapter 3 we will explain which of these five risk management strategies are most important and what commonsense precautions you can take to minimize your general business risks. Chapters 4, 5, and 6 will discuss the special risks involved in three areas of your business—child abuse, travel and transportation, and sick and injured children.

CHAPTER TWO

Getting Started As a Business

Chapter Summary
This chapter explains how to reduce your business risks by complying with your state regulations. It also describes the steps that you should follow to set up your business to operate as safely as possible.

Family child care providers are a special group of individuals who have chosen their profession because they love children. Doing this job properly starts with setting up your business in a way that keeps both you and the children in your care safe. The most important step in doing so is complying with your state's child care regulations. The process of complying with all the licensing rules may take months, and at times it may seem cumbersome; however, bear in mind that these regulations not only protect the children in your care, they also help to protect you. And each year tens of thousands of new providers just like you are able to successfully set up their businesses.

• •

A Licensor by Any Other Name
Every state has its own family child care regulations, and the names of the regulations aren't consistent; they may be referred to as licensing, required and voluntary registration, or self-certification. Since "licensing" is the term that is used most widely, this is the term that is used throughout this book.

• •

Comply with the Child Care Rules and Regulations
Family child care regulations vary widely by state. Before you start caring for children you should contact your county or state social service department to learn about the licensing rules in your area. For example, in some states it's illegal to care for even one child from an unrelated family without having a license. (To find your state's licensing office, go to

www.nncc.org/Evaluation/stlicofc.html. For your state's licensing regulations, go to nrc.uchsc.edu/STATES/states.htm.)

The primary purpose of the state licensing rules is to protect the health and safety of the children, although each state goes about doing this in a different way. Most states prohibit child care providers from using corporal (physical) punishment and 70% of them require providers to be trained in CPR. In Idaho a family child care provider can smoke in front of the children, but most other states prohibit it. There are rules for how long you can leave an infant in a playpen, whether you can accept an ill child into your care, how many hours of training you must take in order to be licensed, what type of immunization records you must keep, how often your home must have a fire inspection, and many more. Some states don't even allow you to use pesticides in areas where the children are present.

Follow the Licensing Rules

The first rule for reducing the risks that you face in your business is to make sure that you're complying with all your state's licensing rules. Obviously, if you don't follow these rules you can lose your license. But more important, if you don't follow them you're putting the children at greater risk for injury and putting yourself at greater risk for a lawsuit. This means that your child care licensor is protecting you as well as the children in your care.

It's in your own best interest to follow all the licensing rules that apply to you. For example, if you have more children in your care than allowed, and an accident occurs in your business, it's more likely that you will be found liable than if you were in compliance with all the regulations. This could mean that you would have to pay hundreds of thousands of dollars in damages because of your failure to follow the rules. In addition, your insurance company might refuse to pay any claims—including your legal fees and damages—that they would otherwise cover, and they could drop your policy when it comes up for renewal.

● ●

Notify Your Licensor If You Move

If you move and continue to operate your business, you should notify your licensor. If you fail to get a license at your new address and start to care for children again, you will be out of compliance and will face greater liability risks.

● ●

Keep Up to Date

Child care licensing rules can change over time, and you need to be sure to keep up with any changes in the laws in your state. For example:

● In 2000 the rules were relaxed in Minnesota so that caregivers could care for more children before they had to be licensed. A year later the rules were changed back to the previous limitations.

● In 2003, after several years of study, there was a major overhaul of the licensing rules in Indiana. Among other changes, newly licensed providers now must submit to a drug test.

Because state rules can evolve over time, it's a good idea to ask your licensor every year if there are any new rules or if any of the old rules have been changed. You need to ask because your licensor probably works with many providers, and if you don't ask her she may not remember if she has already told you about a change.

If your state requires you to renew your license periodically, be sure to renew in a timely fashion. If you don't hear from your licensor when you are up for renewal, contact her. Letting your license expire while you continue to care for children increases your risk of a lawsuit. If a child is injured after your license has expired, it's more likely that you'll be found liable and that your business liability insurance policy may not cover you.

● ●

Follow the Rules about Insurance

Pay particular attention to any licensing rules about insurance. In many states providers who don't have business liability insurance must inform their clients and get a signed statement indicating that the parents understand this.

We strongly recommend that you get adequate business liability insurance, whether it is required or not (see chapter 8). Not having insurance won't prevent a parent from suing you, and not having any money won't prevent a court from ordering you to pay damages (see page 104).

If you choose not to get insurance, it's essential that you carefully follow any state rules about informing the parents. Failing to do this can increase the likelihood that you will be sued, and if you are sued, it will be used against you in the lawsuit.

● ●

Licensing Rules Are Minimum Requirements

Following all your state's licensing rules and regulations isn't the final word in protecting the children or yourself, and by itself it doesn't mean that you're providing high-quality care. For the most part, the licensing rules are intended to establish the minimum health and safety standards needed to protect the children in your care. Providing high-quality care means far more than meeting these minimum standards: it includes offering a developmentally appropriate curriculum for the children and working with the parents to help the children learn.

Anything that you can do to increase your professionalism will increase the quality of your program and help to reduce your business risks. There are several training programs that offer nationally recognized quality standards that are higher than any of the state licensing requirements. In particular, we encourage you to consider the Child Development Associate (CDA), which is a national accreditation program, and the quality standards sponsored by the National Association for Family Child Care (NAFCC). See appendix B for information about these programs.

You can also ask your child care resource and referral agency or your family child care association if there are any other certification or accreditation programs that they would recommend that you participate in.

How Many Children Should You Care For?

To provide a high-quality program and reduce your business risks, you need to be caring for the right number of children. The licensing regulations about the number of children that you can care for are a maximum, not a goal. Not every provider should be caring for the maximum allowed by state law. Evaluate your own goals and your ability to care for the children in your program. Every provider is different in her ability to handle children. You can ask your licensor to help you decide how many children you should care for. Training in child development or child care accreditation can also help you determine the optimal enrollment for your business.

Bear in mind that the number of children you can safely and comfortably care for may change over time. At first you may only feel comfortable caring for three children, but after a year of experience you may decide that you are ready to care for more. If you are going through a stressful period, you may want to consider caring for fewer children for a while.

Don't be influenced by other providers who care for more children than you do and who urge you to do likewise because of the extra income it brings. Also, if you feel that you are fully enrolled, resist the urge to accept another child from a pleading parent who is desperate to find high-quality child care.

If You Are Exempt from Licensing Rules

Many family child care providers don't have to follow their state's licensing regulations; about three-fourths of the states allow providers who only care for a few children to be exempt from their rules. These providers may be called kith and kin, unregulated, or exempt caregivers. Depending on the state, they may include a grandmother who is paid to care for her granddaughter, a caregiver who is caring for five children from one family, or a provider who is caring for up to six children from more than one family.

If you're exempt from the licensing rules, you should take extra steps to keep the children in your care safe. Although you aren't required to do so, you should seriously consider following the same rules that the licensed providers in your state must follow. (To find out your state's rules, ask your licensor or go to nrc.uchsc.edu/STATES/states.htm.)

If you follow your state's strictest health and safety rules, you will decrease the likelihood that accidents will occur or that you will be found liable in a lawsuit. This is especially important if you are exempt from state regulations, because you may not be able to get the same level of insurance protection for your business as a licensed provider (see page 77).

The parents of the children in your care will always appreciate any steps that you take to keep their children safe. In fact, health and safety are usually at the top of the list of what parents look for in choosing a child care provider. If you can show that your program exceeds the state regulations, that you have completed CDA or NAFCC accreditation, or that you have taken other professional training, parents will notice—and they will be willing to pay more for higher-quality care. (For information about how to promote the quality of your program, see the *Family Child Care Marketing Guide*.)

Set Up Your Business Properly

Although it's very important, complying with your state licensing rules is only one of the steps involved in setting up a child care business on a professional basis to minimize your business risks. You will have to fulfill many other business responsibilities in order to protect your family, your business, and the children in your care. Here's a list of the steps that we recommend you take before you start caring for any children:

- Check if there are any legal barriers, such as deed restrictions, homeowners association covenants, or zoning laws, that will affect your ability to run a business in your home (see chapter 14).

- Choose a business structure and set it up (see chapters 16 and 17).

- Register your business name, and find out if you will have to get a business license or pay any business fees (see pages 10–11).

- Check the coverage of your existing insurance policies and buy the appropriate insurance to minimize your business risks and protect your family (see chapters 7–11).

- Write your contract and the specific policies for your program. As described throughout this book, you should have written policies for general and specific field trips (page 43), picking up children (pages 45–48), and privacy (page 121). You will also need a general permission form (page 122) and an emergency plan (page 50), and your contract should include an immunization notice (page 51). (For samples of these forms, see appendix A.)

- Ask your licensor for information about your state's licensing rules and take all the steps needed to comply with them.

- Find out if you will need to take any steps to comply with the Americans with Disabilities Act (see chapter 13).

- In setting your rates, be sure to comply with the price fixing laws (see chapter 13).

All of these topics are discussed in this book; in this chapter we will briefly introduce three issues that you should consider in setting up your business—deed and zoning restrictions, registering your business name, and paying business fees and licenses. For more information on the other steps, see the pages referenced above.

Deed and Zoning Restrictions

Before you start your business you should check to see if any legal restrictions might prevent you from operating a business out of your home or apartment. This topic is covered in detail in chapter 14—but basically, you need to check for any restrictions in the deed to your property, the bylaws of your homeowners association, and local zoning regulations. In addition, don't put up a sign in front of your home without finding out whether the local laws permit this, and if they do, whether they regulate the size and location of the sign (see page 150).

• •

Checklist for Starting a Family Child Care Business

Here's a checklist of the steps needed to set up your business to minimize your risks:

- Check for any legal barriers to operating your business (see chapter 14)
- Set up your business structure (see chapters 16 and 17)
- Register your business name and get a business license (see below)
- Pay business fees (see below)
- Get the proper insurance coverage (see chapters 7–11)
- Write your contracts and policies, including the following:
  - Field trip policy and permission form (page 43)
  - Authorized pickup policy (pages 45–48)
  - Emergency plan (page 50)
  - Sick and injured children policy (page 50) and immunization notice (page 51)
  - SIDS prevention procedures (page 57)
  - Privacy and confidentiality policy (page 121)
  - General permission form (page 122)
- Compile all your plans and policies into an employee manual (pages 25, 36)
- Comply with your state's licensing rules (ask your licensor for information)
- Comply with the ADA (see chapter 13)
- Comply with the price fixing laws (see chapter 13)

• •

Register Your Business Name

Many family child care providers operate under a business name (such as "Dee's Day Care" or "Tender Care for Kids") that they use on their parent contracts, checks, business cards, and so on. If another child care provider begins using the same business name as yours, your program could suffer. To prevent this from happening, you can register your business name with your state (usually with the secretary of state's office). If you live near the border of two states, you may want to register your business name in both states.

In some states you are required to register any business name that you use. In other states you don't need to register your business name if it includes your full name ("Cassandra Bowie's Day Care"), but you do need to register it if it includes only part of your name ("Cassandra's Day Care"). Check with your secretary of state's office for more information. (For a discussion of how to choose a business name, see the *Marketing Guide*.)

Before your state registers your business name, it will check to see that no one else has registered the name that you have chosen. Once your name is registered, no other child care business will be permitted to use it. If you discover that another provider is using your registered name, you can report this to the state, and the state will order her to stop.

If you don't register your business name, another child care provider can register the same name and force you to stop using it, even if you have been using it for many years. This could create considerable confusion for your current and potential clients.

Even if you aren't required to register your business name with your state, we recommend that you do so, because it will help to set a professional tone with your clients. There is a fee to register your business name, but you only have to pay it once, and it is usually less than $50. You can register your business name regardless of how you have structured your business. If you ever want to change your registered business name, you can do so through your secretary of state's office.

Business Fees and Licenses

An increasing number of states are charging family child care providers a child care licensing fee to help offset the cost of the state licensing system. (These fees are 100% tax deductible. However, if you pay a fee to get your license before you start your business, you will need to deduct it over 60 months as a start-up expense—see the *Family Child Care Tax Workbook and Organizer* for more information.)

In addition to a license to practice child care, in some areas family child care providers also have to get a business license before they can operate. This license may be required of all new businesses and there may be a fee involved. Family child care providers who set themselves up as sole proprietors rarely have to get a business license, but it is much more likely to be required if you incorporate, form a partnership, or set up a limited liability company (see chapter 17). Ask your child care licensor or your city or county government if there are any business licenses or fees that apply to your business.

CHAPTER THREE

Reducing General Business Risks

Chapter Summary
This chapter will explain simple ways that you can reduce your business risks by following safe business practices, communicating effectively, and managing your employees carefully.

As explained in chapter 1, there are five strategies that you can use to manage your business risks. However, these strategies aren't equally important. In most cases, there will be few risks that you will be able to avoid, few additional risks that you will take on, and only minor risks that you should retain. This means that your two most important risk-management strategies are reducing your risks and transferring your risks by buying insurance.

This chapter will explain how you can reduce the general risks of operating your business; the next three chapters will explain how to minimize three kinds of major risks. Part II of this book will cover the second important strategy—using insurance to transfer your risks. Insurance is always important, even if you're doing everything you can to reduce your risks.

In explaining how you can reduce the general risks of running a family child care business, this chapter will focus on four commonsense precautions that you can take:

- Follow safe business practices
- Communicate clearly with parents
- Communicate clearly with your licensor
- Carefully screen, train, and monitor your employees

Follow Safe Business Practices
There are three basic business practices that you should get into the habit of following that can significantly reduce many of the business risks described in this book:

- Maintain a safe home
- Follow your safety rules even when parents are present
- Always trust your instincts

Maintain a Safe Home

Keeping your home safe for children is a never-ending task. It's easy for an outlet cover to fall off or to leave a fence gate unlatched. Although it usually comes down to using common sense, even diligent family child care providers can become lax about basic home safety. For example, one study of regulated family child care providers found the following:

- 69% had knives and sharp objects within reach of the children
- 51% had stairs without proper safety gates
- 35% had cleaning supplies that were accessible to the children
- 11% did not have working smoke detectors

However, as a family child care provider, you must maintain constant vigilance about safety. Many of the lawsuits that are brought against family child care providers are based on a failure to keep children safe.

There are many commonsense measures that you can take to keep your home safe. For example, regularly check for safety problems by crawling on your hands and knees around all the areas that the children use, looking for hazards from a child's point of view. Remove or secure the electrical cords to keep the children from tripping or tipping over a lamp or vase. Look for objects that children might try to climb—in one home a child crawled on top of a three-foot bookcase to rest on a pillow and fell, suffering a concussion. Keep potentially hazardous items—such as power tools, outdoor grills, or hot cooking pots—away from the areas where the children play or even pass by.

There is a lot of information available on home safety and health standards. For more suggestions, you can do the following:

- Ask your insurance agent for materials about home safety
- Order the *Family Child Care Health and Safety Video and Checklist* from Redleaf Press
- Order the *Home Safety Checklist* from the American Academy of Pediatrics (see appendix B)
- Ask your licensor, child care resource and referral agency, business liability company, Food Program sponsor, or state Department of Public Safety for home safety information

As a family child care provider, you are responsible for doing everything that you can to protect the safety of the children in your care. In addition to keeping your home safe, this also includes having an emergency plan (see page 50) and an illness policy (see page 50).

Follow Your Safety Rules Even When Parents Are Present

You are responsible for the children in your care until they leave your property, even if their parents are present. In one case, a child's mother would habitually sign her child out at the end of the day, but then stay on to chat with the provider; the child would remain on the provider's property. One day the child got bored, left the house, and got into her mother's car to wait. The mother had left the keys in the ignition; the child put the car in neutral, and the car rolled across the street into a neighbor's front yard. This story could have ended tragically; but fortunately there were no injuries or property damage. However, if there had been, the provider would have been responsible for them.

Many providers are less vigilant about safety when a child's parent is present, because they assume that the parent is responsible for the child's safety. But as long as the parent is on your property, you are likely to be held responsible for anything that happens to the child. This means that you should enforce your own safety rules even after a parent has signed out a child. You should either make sure that the parents leave promptly after picking up their children, or tell them that they must follow your safety rules until they leave your property.

Following your safety rules when parents are present also means enforcing an authorized pickup policy, as described in chapter 5. You shouldn't let a child leave with any adult unless you are certain that adult is authorized to pick up the child, and you need to ensure that the adult transports the child in an appropriate car seat or with seat belts. In addition, if you suspect that anyone who is picking up a child is under the influence of drugs or alcohol, you should take steps to try to prevent the child from leaving with that person (see pages 45–48 for more information).

Always Trust Your Instincts

When dealing with the safety of children, it's important to trust your feelings about whether something is safe. Don't do anything that makes you feel uncomfortable. Parents may make requests that seem reasonable to them but don't feel right to you—a parent may tell you that her child doesn't need a nap, shouldn't play with other children, or needs to bring her own toys into your home. But if you aren't comfortable with a request, don't agree to it.

A family child care provider in California went along with a parent's request to keep a pacifier on a cord around her infant's neck. The child strangled to death, and the resulting claim cost the provider over $850,000.

Many providers have told us that they had a feeling that a parent was going to be a problem during their first interview, and later the parent made an unwarranted claim against them. It's very important to pay attention to your instincts about what's safe—both for the children and for you. Although you may be sorely tempted to enroll a family because you want to care for the child, if you sense that a parent is going to be difficult to deal with, it's usually best to trust your first instincts. Doing so may help you avoid a serious conflict with the parent later.

Communicate Clearly with Parents

When you enroll a new child into your program, you want it to be a long and mutually satisfying relationship for you, the child, and the parent. It's not good for children to move frequently from provider to provider. However, usually the most difficult person to satisfy is the parent, not the child. Use your interview process to screen new families and weed out parents or children who appear to be difficult or inflexible.

Although you can't discriminate against a family because a parent or child has a disability, you can say no if a parent appears to be overly interested in your insurance policies (see chapter 13). Ask for references from the family's previous caregiver. When you call the reference, the best question to ask is whether she would provide care for the family again if she had the chance. (See chapter 12 for more information about confidentiality and how to get references without violating a prospective client's privacy.)

Once you've decided to enroll a family in your program, it's important to establish a regular communication pattern with the parents, starting with your contract and policies. Make sure that you and the parents have a signed copy of the contract, and that you review it together at least once a year. Many parent conflicts occur because one of the parties is not aware of the specific language in the contract. Whenever you change your contract or policies, use that as an opportunity to go over your contract and discuss any concerns that parents have with your rules. (For more information about writing and enforcing your contract, see *Family Child Care Contracts and Policies*.)

Since the parents may not have had much experience with family child care, it's up to you to explain your business rules and expectations. Enforce your rules consistently and establish consequences for failure to comply with them. If a family is late in picking up a child, charge a late fee, or give the parents a warning. If the problem doesn't improve after several warnings, terminate the contract.

In addition to clearly communicating your rules and policies, we recommend that you establish a regular pattern of communicating with parents through daily notes or check-ins. Keeping the parents happy will play a major role in reducing your risks, and one of the best ways to do that is to keep them informed about what is going on with their child. The more you communicate with a parent, the more the parent will trust you.

Prevent Financial Disputes with Parents

Disputes over money are the most common kind of conflict that providers have with parents. We regularly hear about parents who file complaints with their provider's licensor because of a money dispute. Family child care is a major expense for many families, and the stresses of balancing work and family life can lead to conflicts. Also, some parents just aren't comfortable being in a business relationship with the person who is caring for their child.

Since money can be such a highly charged issue, it's critical to communicate the financial commitment outlined in your contract as clearly as you can to parents. You can prevent most conflicts over money and contracts by following some commonsense business practices, including two simple steps:

- Require all parents to pay you at least one week in advance.

- Require parents to give you at least a two-week notice before they leave and to deposit a payment for these last two weeks of care up front. If a parent can't afford to pay the entire deposit at once, set up a payment plan for them.

If you follow these two guidelines, you should never to have to take a parent to court to enforce your contract because the parents of the children in your care will never owe you any money. (Except for the rare case; you may be owed a small amount if a parent who has not finished paying her deposit leaves abruptly soon after enrolling in your program.).

(Low-income parents who are receiving subsidy payments from the county or state probably won't be able to meet these two requirements. If you participate in a state or county financial subsidy program for low-income parents, you must follow the rules of the program. Since these rules may be different from your rules for private-pay parents, be sure to find out what you can and can't do.)

Some providers try to reduce potential conflicts by requiring parents to pay by credit card (your bank can help you set this up) or to participate in electronic payment services that automatically transfer the money from the parent's bank account. (One company that offers this service is Reliafund—www.reliafund.com.)

Get Both Parents to Sign Your Contract

Make sure that both parents understand your rules, even if only one is paying you. Otherwise you may run into a situation in which the other parent picks up the child late and then gets angry when you tell her that you're charging a late fee. If the parents are sharing legal responsibility (custody) for a child, but not living together, it's common for only one parent to be paying the child care provider. However, even if only one parent is paying you, ask to have both parents sign your contract and give both of them a copy of your contract and policies. The parent who isn't paying for your child care services also needs to understand your hours, late fees, vacation policy, and termination policy. We've heard from too many providers who have had difficulties in this situation.

If both parents don't sign your contract and agree to follow your rules, problems can easily arise. For example, the father enrolls the child in your program, signs your contract, and pays your weekly fees. But then one day the mother arrives late for pickup and refuses to pay your late fee. You try to collect the late fee from the dad, but he refuses to pay it, because it was the mother's responsibility. The best way to prevent this is to have a signed contract from each parent and to enforce them separately with each parent.

If the parents have joint legal custody rights, they can both make decisions regarding the child's welfare, including enrolling the child in a child care program. In this case, both parents must be aware of your rules and policies.

If one parent gets angry and starts to take their frustrations out on you, try to resolve the matter with that parent. But if the problem persists, share your concerns with the other parent. Explain that if the situation doesn't improve, you will no longer be able to provide child care services for them. If you let the cooperative parent know that there's a problem that needs to be resolved or they will have to find another provider, they'll find a way to resolve the problem with the other parent.

Document All Injuries to Children

Injuries to children are another area that can lead to disputes and even lawsuits. Check each child for injuries twice a day—when the child arrives in the morning and when the child leaves at the end of the day. During the day, if a child is even mildly injured—for example, by a bump on the head—you need to document what happened and report it to both the parent and your licensor. Often parents will be angrier that you didn't tell them about a child's injury than they would be about the injury itself. (See chapter 4 for a discussion of child abuse and neglect, including your responsibilities as a mandated reporter.)

Whenever you document any injuries to children, it's extremely important to record only your observations, not your opinions or feelings. For example, you should write

> At 3 P.M. on Wednesday, while the children were dancing to music in the playroom, Jennifer fell and bumped her head on the side of the sofa. I examined her head and saw a light red mark about one inch in diameter. The skin was not broken. She cried for about 10 seconds, and then continued to dance with the other children.

Be sure not to add comments such as, "I was very upset when I saw Jennifer fall," or "I was angry at Jennifer because she had been crabby all morning." Any language you use that describes your feelings or your thoughts, rather than simply what you have observed, can be used against you later. The parents can use it as a basis for implying that you were not properly supervising the children.

Ask for Evaluations

Asking parents to fill out an evaluation of your services is another way to improve communication and reduce your risks. We recommend that you ask parents to fill out an evaluation form at least once a year and whenever a family leaves your program. (For a sample evaluation form, see the *Family Child Care Marketing Guide*.) The most important questions that you should ask are the following:

- What do you like best about my program?
- What could I do to improve my program?
- Would you recommend me to another parent? Why or why not?

These evaluations can be very useful. As a rule, most of the responses will be favorable, and if you get a parent's permission, you can use her statements as a reference for prospective parents. You can also use these evaluations to defend yourself against parent complaints.

One provider kept a notebook for comments by her entry and regularly asked the parents to write down any complaints or praise that they had about her program. Later, she had a money dispute with one of the parents, who had never written anything in the book. The parent called her licensor and made many complaints about her. The provider replied that the parent had never shared any of those concerns with her, and showed the licensor her comment notebook. The licensor took this into consideration, and didn't substantiate the complaint. The parent eventually paid the provider what she owed under her contract.

Handling a Disruptive Parent

Conflicts with parents are usually the result of a breakdown in communication, and both sides are responsible for preventing problems from getting out of hand. Resist the temptation to blame parents for any problems that arise. Parents don't usually act irrationally, and sometimes they aren't at fault. When problems arise, make an effort to learn the reasons for the parent's behavior and do what you can to calm things down.

However, sometimes a family child care provider will continue a business relationship with a parent, despite serious conflicts, because she believes that signing a contract with a parent obligates her to provide child care, no matter what happens. However, this is not true—and it increases your risks of doing business.

If a parent is being extremely disruptive (calling you at all hours to complain about minor matters, criticizing you in front of the other parents, or forcing you to make repeated requests before she will sign a permission form) you should consider ending the relationship. A parent who's unhappy with your care, despite your best efforts to resolve the situation, is more likely to file complaints and create trouble.

Of course, you should make every attempt to talk with the parent and work out any problems. But you shouldn't put up with a parent who consistently fails to abide by the rules of your contract or who treats you with disrespect. If this happens, you should terminate your contract with the parent.

Communicate Clearly with Your Licensor

Good communication with your child care licensor can help you reduce your business risks by helping you stay in compliance with the licensing rules. This section will discuss the general issues involved in working with your licensor and dealing with the most common types of problems and complaints. Chapter 4 will explain how to work with your licensor if you are accused of child abuse or neglect. (For more information on working with your licensor, see the *Family Child Care Marketing Guide*.)

Your licensor can be a source of support and expertise in answering your questions and helping you cope with the stress of caring for children. Obviously you will want to develop a good working relationship with her. However, your relationship is a professional one—she is not your friend, she is an agent of the state who is responsible for monitoring the licensing laws. But you will still want to develop a relationship of mutual trust and respect, and the best way to do this is to establish clear communications with each other.

Although it probably wouldn't be appropriate to invite your licensor over for coffee when you start working with her, it is important to maintain a cooperative relationship. If your licensor finds you to be unpleasant or difficult to work with, she may think that you are less professional. If an investigation occurs in which the evidence is your word against the parent's, she may tend to side with the parent. Although this may not seem fair, it is human nature.

As explained on pages 17–18, be sure to report all injuries to children to your licensor, even if this isn't required by your state's rules. Some states only require you to report an incident if the child has to seek medical attention. However, you should report all incidents because you never know how serious an injury may be. In one case, a child fell on his provider's staircase and hit his head, leaving a large bruise. The parents seemed to understand that it was an accident. But later that night at home the child started vomiting and had to be taken to the emergency room. The next day the provider received a call from her licensor wondering what had happened and why she hadn't reported the injury.

It's always best for your licensor to hear your side of the story first. The parent will usually get their version of the story from the child. A young child may not clearly communicate the whole story, and the parents will be free to fill in the gaps with their own imagination. (For an explanation of how to report and document injuries, see page 18.)

Complaints

In most states, when anyone makes a complaint about your program, your licensor will investigate and conclude that the complaint was substantiated (it happened), unsubstantiated (it wasn't proven), or unfounded (it didn't happen). In each case, a record of the complaint may be put in your file. Although you should be notified of any complaints, it's a good idea to ask your licensor if you can review your file at least once a year. (Allow the agency time to prepare your file for review.)

Each state has its own privacy rules about what information in your files can be viewed by you and what can be viewed by other people. It's important to find out what parents would be able to see in your file. If you believe that the information in your file is inaccurate or incomplete, ask if you can add a note to the file that explains your side of the story.

Since many parents aren't familiar with the licensing process, they may not understand the difference between a substantiated and unsubstantiated complaint. They may assume that every complaint in your file is true. You should ask your licensor what she would say about you if a parent calls to inquire. Ask her how she would explain any substantiated or unsubstantiated complaints in your file. If you aren't happy with her response, you can ask her to use language that is more favorable to you. If she won't, then ask if you can add your own notes to the file, and ask her to refer parents to these notes.

Licensing Rules

If a parent files a complaint, or if your licensor visits your home and notices something amiss, you have a right to know what rule you are accused of violating. However, some licensing rules are subject to different interpretations, and you may need to discuss them with your licensor to clarify what they mean.

For example, many states have a rule that family child care providers must be within "sight or sound" of the children at all times. But what does this mean? Can you allow a child to play at the end of your backyard, hundreds of feet away? Can you use an electronic device to monitor children who are sleeping in a basement bedroom? Some licensors might interpret this rule to mean that you must always be close enough to intervene and prevent serious injury.

If you aren't sure what a rule means, ask your licensor for clarification. You can also talk with the licensor's supervisor or ask your licensor to submit your request to the state department of licensing for clarification. (Some states will allow you to seek a variance for some licensing rules; your licensor should be able to explain this.) If the issue is important to other family child care providers, get your association involved in the process.

However, in the end, you must obey all licensing rules. If you believe that a rule is unfair or obsolete, you can lobby your state legislature to change the law.

Your Licensor Plays Two Roles

Your licensor plays two different roles when she is talking with you about your business—she may be acting either as your licensor or as your advisor. She is acting as your licensor when she tells you that you are in violation of a particular rule, such as not keeping poisons locked up or not washing your hands after changing a diaper. However, she can also act as your advisor and give you advice about how to better care for children.

In this role, she may offer recommendations such as, "I think you should have the children eat in the dining room rather than the kitchen, because the dining room is a much friendlier room for them," or "Why don't you play classical music for your babies? I hear that it's good for them."

You aren't required to follow any suggestions that your licensor gives you when she's acting as an advisor, because she isn't accusing you of violating any licensing rule. If you aren't clear which hat your licensor is wearing, ask her. If she admits that she's acting as your advisor, and you don't wish to take her advice, then politely thank her for her suggestion, and do what you want.

Rule Violations

If your licensor says that you are in violation of a rule, she will most likely write up a report that will specify exactly what rule you broke. However, this may not happen in every case. Here are some examples:

- A provider had a financial dispute with a parent who left abruptly. Afterward her licensor received multiple complaints from the parent, alleging that the provider didn't have age-appropriate toys and activities, was guilty of poor supervision, and had disciplined her one-year-old inappropriately. The licensor was only able to substantiate the complaint about discipline. The provider admitted that she had given the one-year-old a timeout, and the licensor cited her for disciplining a child who was too young. But when the provider asked what licensing rule she was accused of violating, the licensor and her supervisor were unable to locate such a rule. As a result, the licensor withdrew the violation citation against the provider.

- Another provider who was homeschooling her own children was told by her licensor that the law forbade her from conducting another occupation during child care hours. The licensor had determined that homeschooling was an occupation. The provider said that she worked with her own children only in the evenings or on weekends. The licensor asked the provider to sign a letter stating that she would not homeschool during child care hours. After consulting with an attorney, the provider asked the licensor why she had to sign a letter stating she would follow the state law, when she wasn't being asked to do the same thing for any other state law. After considering this, the licensor backed off and withdrew her request for a signed letter.

Whenever a licensor tells you that you are in violation of a rule, you should always ask to see the exact language of the rule. If the licensor's interpretation of the rule is not the same as yours, ask for clarification from the licensor's supervisor.

In addition, never sign a licensor's inspection report if it doesn't spell out exactly what the licensor observed during the inspection. If you ever end up appealing an action against you, vague language (such as, "the house was messy" or "the children weren't properly supervised") will be difficult to refute. It could also be used against you in a lawsuit, if a parent were to sue you.

If a licensor tells you that you are being investigated because of a parent complaint dealing with the supervision of children, contact your insurance agent. Your insurance agent may be able to offer you advice on how to prepare for a potential lawsuit. (See chapter 11 for a discussion of how to work with your insurance agent to protect yourself from risks.)

Some family child care providers are very sensitive about any complaints about their program, no matter how small. We have spoken with many providers who were extremely upset after being cited for a small licensing violation. If you pride yourself on offering quality care, you may be hurt and embarrassed about this, even though the consequences are minor. We encourage you not to be too hard on yourself if this happens to you. No one is perfect. Let it go, and move on to the more important things in life.

If you violate a licensing rule that is more substantial, you may have to take some type of corrective action, such as removing a dangerous item or more closely watching the children when they play outside. In serious cases you may be put on probation, suspension, or have your license revoked. If this happens, you may want to appeal the action taken against you and consult an attorney (see chapter 15). Your licensor should be able to answer any questions about your rights to appeal her decisions. Bear in mind that to exercise those rights you will have to meet any deadlines that are involved in the process.

Dealing with a Difficult Licensor

Maintaining a professional relationship with your licensor will benefit you by helping to manage your business risks. It would be a miracle if every relationship between provider and licensor went smoothly. Fortunately, the most common problems are personality differences and minor conflicts that can be managed without too much difficulty. However, more serious problems can also arise, and there are rare cases where a licensor is unreasonable or difficult to work with.

You have the right to be treated with respect by your licensor, and she should always be reasonable in her dealings with you. She probably has the right to drop in to visit your program unannounced. However, if she's been questioning you for two hours, and you need to make lunch, or take a break, it's reasonable to expect her to allow this. In addition, it's always reasonable to request that someone else be present during any interview with your licensor.

If you have made every effort to work with your licensor and you feel that she is hostile or unprofessional, you can ask to speak to her supervisor and request a new licensor. If other providers in your area have had similar problems with this licensor, you may want to involve them in your discussions with the supervisor. One family child care association went to the extreme step of complaining about a licensor to the state licensing board; they were able to have the licensor removed.

However, these kinds of situations are very unusual. Nearly every problem you might have with your licensor can be resolved through direct communication with her. Bear in mind that she has dealt with many other family child care providers, some of whom may not have been as reasonable as you. A licensor who has had a bad experience with another provider may be nervous or cautious in her interactions with you. Take this into consideration and make an effort to reach out to her. If you need help dealing with your licensor, ask for support from your fellow providers or your child care resource and referral agency.

Carefully Screen, Train, and Monitor Your Employees

Although you may not think of yourself as an employer, you are responsible for the actions of anyone who helps you in your business, whether or not you pay that person for the work. It's extremely important to understand the risks that you incur when someone works in your business. No matter who is assisting you—or whether that person is a paid worker, an unpaid worker, or an independent contractor—in virtually every situation you will be assuming at least some liability for that person's actions and welfare.

There are four major issues that you need to understand in order to manage the risks associated with having someone else work in your business:

- You assume a general liability risk whenever you allow anyone else to work in your business or interact with the children in your care.
- You need to make sure that any worker (paid or unpaid) who comes into contact with the children in your care is covered by your business liability and business property insurance policies (see chapters 7, 8, and 9).
- You need to buy workers' compensation insurance for all workers who are covered by your state workers' compensation regulations (chapter 9).
- You need to understand the IRS (and your state's) definition of employees and comply with the tax and reporting requirements that apply to them (page 87).

Chapters 8 and 9 will explain how to buy insurance to protect yourself against the liabilities that you assume when you hire employees, and how to make sure that they are covered in your policies. Chapter 9 will discuss workers' compensation insurance and the IRS definition of employees. For more information about screening employees, see pages 35–36.

The biggest general liability risks that you face as an employer are the possibility that a worker might injure herself or a child. If this happens, you are likely to be responsible for the injured party's medical expenses and could also be found liable if the parents were to sue you. This section will explain how you can minimize your general liability risks by carefully hiring, training, and supervising your employees. However, since the same risks apply to anyone who works in your business, paid or unpaid, you should also apply these practices to any unpaid helpers.

The Hiring Process

Before you start the process of hiring anyone to help you in your business, there are some things that you should check:

- Ask your insurance agent whether your business liability policy (see chapter 8) provides coverage for child abuse by all your employees or unpaid workers. Some insurance policies won't cover volunteers or temporary employees. If you don't have this coverage, get it. If you don't have it, you shouldn't allow anyone else to work in your business.
- Contact your licensor and ask if there are any state regulations about the qualifications of the workers you hire. Your state may also require background checks.
- Find out if you are subject to any deed restrictions, homeowners association covenants, or zoning laws that might restrict your right to hire employees (see chapter 14).

To locate potential employees, you could try the following approaches:

- Contact the career program at your local high school and ask if they offer work-study courses in child development. If they do, the students might be able to work in your business for credit. Students are likely to be eager to perform well, since they are being evaluated by both you and their teacher.
- Contact child development teachers at the local community colleges and ask if they know of any potential employees for your business.
- Ask your licensor or other providers you know who have hired employees if they can refer you to any potential employees.

Once you have identified and interviewed some candidates, carefully screen those you are interested in before you decide whom to hire:

- Do a criminal background check, whether or not it is required by your state.
- Do a credit check through a credit bureau (see appendix B).
- Ask for past work references and check them thoroughly. You may have difficulty getting much information from previous employers; the key question to ask is whether the employer would hire this person again.
- Ask for references from previous coworkers or the parents of children for whom the person has provided care.
- Examine the person's education credentials. All your employees should take first aid and CPR training before they begin work, if they haven't done so already.

You should be able to get some guidelines on the legal requirements for hiring (and firing) employees from your state attorney general's office. For example, in making your hiring decisions, you may or may not be legally allowed to consider factors such as race, national origin, age, sex, religion, or disability (see chapter 13). However, even if state or federal law allows you to discriminate, we don't recommend that you do so.

Training and Monitoring Employees

Once you have hired someone, contact your licensor, the parents in your program, and your insurance agent; inform them who this person is and what she will be doing in your program. Although your employee may already have experience with children, she must agree to follow the rules of your program. Be sure to communicate the rules of your program clearly to new employees in an employee manual (also see page 36) that includes your rules for the following:

- Supervising children
- Disciplining children
- Emergency procedures
- Infection control measures
- Who is authorized to pick up children
- State-mandated reporting laws
- Privacy and confidentiality
- The special needs of individual children (food allergies, medications, and so on)

Don't assume that your employees know what you are thinking; encourage them to ask you questions if they don't understand something about your rules. When you change any of your rules, clearly state your new expectations. Encourage all your employees to take regular training courses in child development.

Carefully Monitor All Employees

To reduce your business risks, it's essential to carefully monitor all your employees by supervising, observing, and evaluating them on a regular basis:

- **Supervise:** Closely supervise your employees to make sure they are following your rules. Be especially alert for any indications that the employee may not be doing everything possible to keep the children safe.

- **Observe and document:** Observe how your employees interact with the children. Is their behavior appropriate? Is the language that they use in front of the children appropriate? Document your observations on a regular basis.

- **Evaluate:** Evaluate the work of your employees at least once every six months. Share with the employee your observations, concerns, and suggestions for improvement, and give praise for work well done.

CHAPTER FOUR

Child Abuse

Chapter Summary
This chapter discusses the issues of child abuse and neglect, including your responsibilities as a mandated reporter and how to protect yourself against allegations of child abuse.

Child abuse and neglect is a national tragedy that affects more than one million children a year. Although most instances of child abuse occur in the child's own home, rather than in a child care program, you have a legal responsibility to report suspected cases of child abuse, and you are also in a position to help keep the children in your care safe. You also need to be alert to the possibility that a client-parent could make an accusation of child abuse against you or another member of your family. This chapter will explain how you can protect both yourself and the children in your care from these risks.

No one likes to think that child abuse might become an issue in her child care program. However, this is a serious matter that requires you to do all that you can to protect both the children and yourself. Although the close relationships you develop with parents may make it difficult to report your suspicions, remember that the child's welfare always comes first.

Taking the reasonable steps of a caring professional includes fulfilling your responsibilities as a mandated reporter, getting adequate business liability insurance to protect yourself, and seeking legal help if necessary.

(Portions of this section are based on materials published by the Child Care Law Center. For more information, see appendix B.)

You Are a Mandated Reporter
As a family child care provider, you have a special legal responsibility to protect children—every state has laws that require family child care providers to report any known or suspected cases of child abuse or neglect. These laws generally give family child care providers the special legal status of "mandated reporters" of child abuse and neglect. (Child care licensors are also mandated reporters.)

Although the child abuse reporting laws vary by state, they usually require you to report to the authorities if you are aware or have reason to believe that a child is being neglected or abused or has been abused or neglected in the past. Failure to meet these reporting obligations can result in loss of your license, a civil fine, money damages, or even time in jail.

It's important to inform parents of your mandatory reporting responsibilities when they enroll their children in your program, since this legal obligation supersedes their rights for privacy and confidentiality (see chapter 12).

● ●

Help Educate Parents about Child Abuse

As a family child care provider, you are in a unique position to observe children and help parents cope with the sometimes stressful and difficult experience of parenting. For example, you may want to consider these suggestions:

- Be a sympathetic listener and offer encouragement and support to parents.
- Model good child care techniques to show parents how to handle everyday conflicts.
- Ask your local child protection office or child care resource and referral agency for materials that offer information to parents for preventing child abuse. Share this information with the parents of the children in your care.
- Locate classes in your area on parenting and guiding children, and share this information with the parents of the children in your care.
- Contact your child care resource and referral agency or your United Way agency for information about local resources for families.

● ●

What Are You Required to Report?

It's extremely important that you understand your responsibilities under your state's mandated reporting law. Be sure to request a copy of the law—or at least a summary of its key points—from your licensor, county child protection office, or local child care resource and referral agency. You need to know your state's mandated reporting law because there are severe consequences for failing to follow it.

Your state may require you to report various kinds of abuse, including physical abuse, sexual abuse, neglect, and emotional abuse. Although the legal definitions of these categories can differ, here are some general guidelines:

- Physical abuse is causing injury to a child by hitting, kicking, shaking, bruising, beating, or burning.
- Sexual abuse is any sexual activity between a child and an adult, including exposure, displaying pornography, fondling, or overt sexual acts.

- Neglect is a condition in which a child's basic needs for food, shelter, clothing, or prompt medical attention are not met. It may include inadequate supervision, refusal to seek medical care, or extreme spousal abuse in the child's presence. Neglect can be something that a parent or caregiver fails to do for a child.
- Emotional abuse is behavior—either an overt act or a failure to act—that causes a child serious behavioral, cognitive, emotional, or mental disturbance. It can include habitual belittling or scapegoating, refusing medical treatment, or extreme and inappropriate punishment (such as confining a child in a dark closet).

Some states extend their reporting requirements to all the children that a family child care provider comes into contact with, not just the children in her care. Also, most states allow parents to use corporal punishment (physical discipline, such as spanking) with their own children, but outlaw it for family child care providers, even with parental consent.

In most cases, you will have a legal responsibility to report suspected abuse within a specific deadline to your child protection office. You may be required to report within hours of becoming aware of the problem and to submit a written report within a few days. If you aren't sure what your state law requires, call your child protection office and ask. Although your licensor can be helpful in understanding your mandated reporting responsibilities, your state's child protection office has the final word in interpreting the law.

● ●

If Your Own Child Is a Babysitter

If your own child works as a babysitter, be aware that babysitters may also have responsibilities as a mandated reporter of child abuse and neglect under your state law. In addition, in some states the children of family child care providers are prohibited from working as a babysitter in the provider's home "after hours." Ask your licensor about the rules in your state.

● ●

When Should You Report Child Abuse?

If you know, or reasonably suspect, that child abuse has occurred, you probably have a legal responsibility to report it. Whenever you first report an incident of child abuse, be sure to also contact your licensor as a means of protecting yourself. If you have reason to believe that a child is in immediate physical danger, contact your local police. If you are unsure where or how to report the problem, call your licensor, your child protection office, or your local child care resource and referral agency.

In some cases, you may have reason to suspect that child abuse has occurred, but without proof, you may be afraid that if you report the suspected abuse and it isn't true, the parents might sue you. Virtually all state laws give mandated reporters immunity for any report that is filed in good faith. *Immunity* means that any lawsuit against you will be thrown out of court, so you should have no fear about being sued. If you are sued anyway, contact your insurance agent to see if your business liability policy offers legal assistance. Then consult with an attorney, who will probably get the case dismissed immediately.

When you make a report, the child protection office is supposed to keep your name confidential. However, because of the close relationships between parents and caregivers, it's quite possible that the parent will be able to determine that you were the one who reported the abuse. Even so, this is not a reason to ignore your responsibility as a mandated reporter.

● ●

Reporting Injuries While a Child Is in Your Care

If a child is accidentally injured while in your care, the first thing you should do is seek medical treatment. But it's also extremely important that you report any accidents to your child care licensor as soon as possible. Quick reporting can help protect you against accusations of child abuse or negative licensing actions.

In one case, a provider in Alabama was changing a baby's diaper on the bed when she was distracted by another child. As the baby started slipping off the bed, she instinctively grabbed for the baby and caught her by the leg before her head hit the floor. In doing so, she caused a fracture of the baby's leg. She immediately called for medical help and began providing first aid; then she called the parents and her licensor. During the investigation that followed, the fact that she had called her licensor so quickly was cited as an important reason why no negative action was taken against her.

● ●

Reporting Child Abuse

Filing a report about suspected child abuse or neglect is very stressful for everyone involved. However, you shouldn't hesitate to contact your licensor or child protection worker if you have any suspicions that a child has been maltreated. Examine the children in your care when they arrive in your home, and if you observe an injury you should report it promptly to your licensor. You want to avoid the problem of not reporting a child's injury and having the parent make a false accusation against you later.

Many states require providers to report injuries to children. Your licensor can answer your questions and help you determine if the injury represents a reportable case of maltreatment, and if so, how to report it. You should also feel free to contact your local child protection office directly with any questions or suspicions. You can ask for this advice without revealing your name. If you don't feel comfortable about the advice that is being given to you by a child protection worker, ask to talk to that person's supervisor.

It's often a good idea to talk with the parents first to see if there is a reasonable explanation of the child's injuries (there usually is). However, it isn't a good idea to investigate your suspicions further by interviewing the child (beyond a few simple questions) or talking with the other parents or children. Don't try to investigate whether the child abuse actually occurred—this isn't your role, and any actions that you take could hinder the investigation, influence the testimony of other people, or affect the credibility of their testimony. However, despite the parents' explanations and your licensor's advice, in the end you will need to rely on your own best judgment about whether there is enough evidence that you are required to report the situation.

Although it's never easy, if you do decide to report a suspected case of child abuse or neglect after careful consideration, bear in mind that your goal is to act in the best interests of the child. If you need support during this experience, don't hesitate to ask for help from your family, your religious community, or other professionals. However, if you do seek help or counseling, you must keep any information confidential that might identify the family or the child involved (see chapter 12).

• •

Don't Ignore Your Instincts

A provider who had over 17 years of experience shared the following story about her first encounter with suspected child abuse. One of her first clients was the mother of a three-year-old girl. The girl's parents were going through a bitter divorce, and the provider had a strange feeling about the father. She couldn't identify exactly what was wrong, but she noticed that the little girl behaved dramatically different after visits with him. She told the mother about her feelings, but didn't pursue it further. Soon afterward the mother moved away, and the girl left her care.

Fourteen years later she ran into the mother in a store. The mother approached her and thanked her for sharing her suspicions. They had been correct—the father had been sexually abusing the girl, but the mother hadn't been able to get enough evidence to convict him until the girl was eight years old. Her daughter was now a teenager, struggling in high school, feeling depressed, and experimenting heavily with drugs.

The provider wondered if this story might have ended differently if she had reported her "uneasy feelings" to child protection. And indeed, it could well have made a difference if she had reported her suspicions and asked for advice.

• •

After You File a Report

Many family child care providers wonder whether they should tell the child's parents that they have filed a child abuse report. However, before you say anything, you need to ask child protection if it's okay to tell the parents. If they tell you not to say anything, you must comply with their instructions. The child protection office may ask you not to tell anyone about the maltreatment report.

If the child protection office says that it's okay to tell the parents, it will be up to you. Although you may wish to be open about what you have done, discussing the report with the parents may raise further issues. (It will be easier to handle this kind of situation if you have clearly explained your responsibilities as a mandated reporter when families enroll in your program.)

If you decide to tell the parents, they are likely to become angry or defensive and may decide to terminate their relationship with you immediately. Try to keep calm and not respond with anger. If you aggravate the situation, the parent may file a complaint against you or make other threats. You should simply remind them of your legal responsibilities as a mandated reporter and explain that you had no choice. You might offer to explain the investigation process to them if you are familiar with it.

The Investigation Process

Once you have made a report, the authorities will decide whether to conduct an investigation. If they do, your state laws will dictate what follows next. The investigation may be conducted by the police, the child protection office, your child care licensor, or all three. Their job will be to determine if the child has been maltreated, and, if so, what action should be taken to protect the child and punish the wrongdoer.

Depending on the circumstances, the investigators may interview you, the child, the child's parents, the other parents in your program, other observers, and perhaps other members of your family. The child may be removed from your care. It is important that you cooperate fully with the investigators who contact you and follow their directions about what you can and cannot say to the other parents of the children in your care. You cannot be held liable for anything that you say to investigators, and any information that you provide should be kept confidential.

As a mandated reporter you are likely to be told if your report is accepted for investigation, and later you may be given a summary of the outcome of the investigation. However, you will probably be told little else. Your state law will determine how much information you can receive, and if you want more information you can ask to see a copy of the law governing release of information to mandated reporters.

Document the Incident and the Investigation

Keep your own records of the incident and its aftermath in a single file apart from your other records (in case it is requested as evidence later). This file should include your notes about what you saw that led you to make the report, and a summary of all your conversations that relate to the case with investigators, your licensor, the parents of the child, other parents, and anyone else. These records may help you remember what happened if you are later called to testify in court, or if accusations are later made against you.

In your file, record only the facts of what you heard people say or what you observed someone do. Do not write down your thoughts, opinions, or feelings; it's possible that you may eventually have to turn over your notes to a judge, and any comments about your thoughts and feelings could weaken your evidence or be turned against you. If you become concerned at any time that the investigation might start to focus on you or another member of your family, you should consult an attorney.

Protecting Yourself from Allegations of Child Abuse

It is an unfortunate fact that family child care providers are vulnerable to false accusations of child abuse or neglect. A disgruntled parent may accuse you, or members of your family, of inadequate supervision, disregard for safety measures, inappropriate behavior, or physical or sexual abuse. However, there are several steps that you can take to protect yourself and your family from these risks:

- Stay informed about child development
- Know your state's child care regulations
- Monitor your own stress level
- Communicate clearly with parents
- Carefully screen your employees
- Document your observations
- Keep your licensor informed

You can also ask your licensor for help in identifying other procedures that you should follow to protect yourself. Two of these points—communicate clearly with parents and carefully screen potential employees—also play an important role in reducing your general business risks, and they are described from that perspective in chapter 3. They are explained here in the context of protecting yourself from child abuse, but see chapter 3 for more information.

Stay Informed about Child Development

Keep yourself and your employees informed about normal child development and how to use positive discipline methods (for more information, see appendix B). Based on this, develop policies for your business that cover how to handle developmental issues such as sexual play between children, toileting, diaper changing, positive discipline, and appropriate touching.

We recommend that you never use any kind of corporal punishment (physical discipline) for any reason. Most states prohibit you from doing this, and even if it is permitted by your state, you should avoid it for your own protection (as well as concern for its effect on children). For example, in Nebraska it's legal for you to use corporal punishment if the parent signs a permission form. However, a parent may later change her mind or say that she didn't realize what she was signing. Then she may decide to sue you.

It is unwise to allow children to play unattended at any time. Leaving children unsupervised increases the chances that they will behave inappropriately toward each other or be treated inappropriately by someone else. Limit the number of places where children can hide, and leave nap room doors open.

• •

Sexual Play

Allegations of sexual abuse can sometimes arise out of children's sexual play. If a child's behavior goes over the line, ask your licensor for guidance. If you believe that a child may have been abused by another child, you must report this to the proper authorities, as a mandated reporter.

Parents have differing attitudes toward sexual play and experimentation in children. To protect yourself, you need to be informed about normal sexual development. You may want to give the parents of the children in your care some materials that explain normal behavior. Discuss their concerns and questions, and explain your policies and views. Report any strong reaction from a parent to your licensor.

• •

Know Your State's Child Care Regulations

Your state's child care regulations are there to protect you, as well as the children in your care. You need to understand all the licensing regulations that apply to you and stay in compliance with them. To avoid allegations of abuse, it's especially important to follow the regulations about corporal punishment. If a parent wants you to spank her child when he misbehaves, and your state law forbids this, you must follow the law, even if it means losing that parent as a client.

Whenever you interview a new family, observe the child and the parents for any behavior that makes you feel uncomfortable and any signs of abuse or neglect. For example, you may feel that the parents are too aggressive toward you or too harsh with their child. If you're at all uncomfortable with the family's behavior, you can refuse to accept the child, even if you don't feel that there's any reasonable grounds to suspect child abuse.

Although you aren't allowed to reject a family on the basis of race, religion, disability, and so on (see chapter 13), you are allowed to turn them down because you feel uncomfortable with their behavior.

If you aren't sure about a family, you could take the child on for a two-week trial period during which either party can end the relationship on a day's notice. This will allow you and the parents to feel each other out to see if you are a good match.

Monitor Your Own Stress Level

A stressed child care provider is more likely to make errors in judgment or abuse children. Monitor your own stress level, and if you feel that you are experiencing a lot of stress caring for the children, consider reducing the number of children in your program.

Communicate Clearly with Parents

To keep parents from misunderstanding your words or actions, it's helpful to talk with them regularly about your child care practices. Be sure to communicate in a positive, open manner that invites comments or questions. When problems arise, it's important that you share openly with the parents what happened, what you did about it, and why. If a parent doesn't have enough time to talk with you when she drops off or picks up her child, set up a regular time to talk on the phone in the evening.

•••

Media Violence, Video Games, and Pornography
You should be sensitive to how parents might react to seeing any magazines or other materials containing sexual or violent content in your home, including R-rated movies on cable television or pornographic images on a computer. Some parents may not want their young children to watch PG or PG-13 movies or certain television shows.

If you care for older children who use the Internet in your home, develop policies about what sites they can visit, and use parental blocking software to enforce it. Also try to block unsolicited e-mails that contain sexual content or links to pornographic Web sites. If you have trouble blocking these messages, talk to your licensor about how to handle this.

Some video games contain graphic images and violence, and some music that older children listen to might contain lyrics that are violent or inappropriate for younger children. You need to monitor all the games and music that are played in your home.

•••

Carefully Screen Your Employees
You can be held liable for any injuries to children caused by your employees. This potential liability extends to part-time substitutes, occasional help, and even volunteers who help you with the children. Anyone who works with the children in your program can create a potential liability problem for you, regardless of whether you pay that person or withhold payroll taxes.

To reduce the risks of liability make sure you use a high degree of care in selecting the person or persons who will be with the children. (For more information about hiring employees, see chapter 3.) Follow any state rules about criminal background checks, check references, and use your independent judgment about the person's qualifications to work with children.

When considering an employee, look for any signs, even subtle, of emotional problems, substance abuse, sexual difficulties, poor judgment, and insensitivity or harshness toward children. For further information on the hiring process, see the publication by John Patterson listed in appendix B.

Before you hire your first employee, you should follow these guidelines from "Child Care and Child Abuse" (see appendix B):

- Write an employee manual (see page 25). Include your state's laws about corporal punishment, and state that violating these laws will be grounds for termination. If your state doesn't have a law against corporal punishment, you can still have a strict policy against it. Your policy should also spell out your state's child abuse mandated reporting law. Your employee probably has a duty to report known or suspected child abuse to the authorities, even if you disagree with her. You can't retaliate against an employee who makes a report.

- Share your health, safety, and emergency procedures with your employees. Make sure that your employees understand who is authorized to pick up each child and any special custody arrangements for the children in your care.

- Give your employees training (or send them to workshops) on child abuse and neglect, CPR, child development, and appropriate discipline measures.

- Closely supervise your employees and conduct regular reviews of their performance. Be sure to discuss stress and how to reduce it. (See chapter 3.)

- Consider adopting national quality standards for your program (such as accreditation by the National Association for Family Child Care).

- Pursue specialized training for yourself or your staff, such as a Child Development Associate (CDA) credential.

- Make sure that your business liability insurance policy covers acts by your employees and anyone else who helps in your business. If it doesn't, switch to a policy that does.

Document Your Observations

In investigating an allegation of child abuse, the authorities may only have the unsupported evidence of two people—you and the child's parent. Keeping written documentation is a form of self-defense that can make a critical difference in a case such as this. Your notes should only include the facts that you observed, not your opinions or feelings. If an accusation goes to court, you could be forced to turn over your records, and any subjective comments could weaken your evidence or be used against you. We recommend that you create a file for each child and keep in it the following records:

- Notes that summarize your oral or written communications with the parents about any serious conflicts, discussions about the care of their child, or other disputes with parents.

- Copies of any accident reports or other records that you filed with your licensing agency for incidents that happened to a child alone, between children, or between adults and children. If there were any adult witnesses, get a written statement of what they observed.

- Your observations each day of any marks or bruises that were present when the child arrived in your home. If the parent or another adult is present when you see these marks or bruises, ask that person to sign a note indicating that the marks or bruises were present. Some providers ask parents to sign a statement when they sign out their child each day that the child is in good health and doesn't have any marks or bruises.

- Your notes that document the child's behavior problems and your efforts to address them.

- Photographs of any unexplained injuries. You may be able to take these pictures without the parent's permission, as long as they are used only as evidence in a later investigation by authorities. Check with your licensor about this. (See chapter 12 for more information about privacy issues.)

Keep Your Licensor Informed

If a parent who is upset with you because of a contract dispute makes a complaint against you to licensing or child protection services, child protection and your licensor will screen the complaint, and if they don't think the accusation is serious, they may take no action. But if the complaint is serious, they may initiate an investigation that can greatly disrupt your life, even if they conclude later that the complaint was unfounded.

You can help inoculate yourself against unfounded complaints by keeping your licensor informed about all conflicts that arise with parents. You may wish to write a note about any major conflicts and mail it to her so that there is a record in your files. Make it a practice to always contact your licensor in the following situations:

- You have a serious disagreement with a parent
- You are about to give a termination notice to a parent, and you believe that the parent will take it badly
- An unhappy parent terminates your care
- Any circumstance in which you feel threatened by a parent

If your licensor hears from you first about a conflict with a parent, she will be much more likely to give you the benefit of the doubt if she later receives a complaint from that parent. This is particularly true if the licensor is aware that there has been a financial conflict with the parent. Licensors are less likely to take a complaint seriously if they believe that the parent is simply seeking revenge for a dispute over money.

• •

State Laws Vary

This chapter discusses the general legal and regulatory principles that apply to child abuse and neglect. Since the state laws on these issues can vary greatly, we recommend that you check with an advisor who is familiar with your state law before you take any action.

• •

What to Do If You Are Accused of Child Abuse

Even if you follow all the preventative steps outlined above, there is no guarantee that some-one will not make an accusation against you for maltreating a child. If this does happen, it's normal to feel shock, anger, hurt, and betrayal. In this crisis, you may have a sense that everything is out of control and fear what will happen next. Understanding the process of a child abuse investigation can help to ease some of these fears. Although each state has its own procedures, here is a general description of what generally happens.

An accusation of child abuse may trigger an investigation by three groups—the police, child protection services, and child care licensing. Each agency may conduct a separate investigation, or they may coordinate their efforts. The role of each group is quite different, and it's important to understand the possible outcomes of each group's investigation.

The Role of Child Protection

Child protection services is responsible for protecting children from abuse. Their investigation will be focused on determining whether maltreatment took place. If they find that it did, their information will be turned over to the police for possible criminal charges and to child care licensing for possible negative licensing action. If there is an accusation against you for abusing your own child, child protection services can order you to seek counseling, or—in very serious cases—take the child away from you.

The Role of the Police and the Courts

The police are responsible for enforcing the law and recommending whether to file criminal charges against those who violate them. Their investigation will be focused on determining whether you have broken the law. If you are convicted of a criminal charge, you can be fined money damages, spend time in jail, or both. A high standard of proof must be met before you can be convicted of criminal charges, and usually the facts must show guilt beyond a reasonable doubt.

The Role of Licensing

The child care licensing agency is responsible for regulating the health and safety of the children who are enrolled in family child care programs. If a parent makes serious allega-tions against you, your licensor will assist the police and child protection services in their investigations. If they find a violation of the licensing rules, the agency can take a range of corrective actions, from a simple demand to change a practice to more serious steps such as probation, suspension, and revocation of your license.

The standard of proof that a licensing agency needs to apply corrective action is lower than that required by a criminal case. In general, your licensor can take action based on a preponderance of the evidence. In other words, the agency simply needs to determine that the abuse "more likely than not" happened. This difference between a criminal investigation and a licensing investigation can be difficult to understand. It means that even if there isn't enough evidence to bring a criminal case, or if you are found innocent in court, you could still lose your license.

How to Protect Yourself

Not all allegations of child abuse result in an investigation. If the complaint is perceived as minor, child protection services or licensing may drop the matter after a short consideration

If an investigation is initiated against you, it's likely that you will only find out when an investigator contacts you by phone or in person and starts asking you questions. You may be questioned by a police officer, a child protection worker, or your licensor. These agencies may interview some or all of the families in your care, families who have left your care, other members of your family, and any other witnesses. They may or may not notify the families in your care about the allegations, depending on their seriousness.

It will likely take the investigators months to finish gathering facts, and you may or may not be allowed to continue caring for children while the investigation is going on. Eventually, the investigation will be completed and decisions will be made about what action will be taken by the various agencies. But in the meantime, there are some things that you should be doing to protect yourself:

Seek Legal Help

Since accusations of child abuse can have very serious consequences, you should seek professional legal help as soon as you discover that an investigation is under way. Some providers, knowing that the accusation against them is false, may hesitate to hire a lawyer because they can't imagine that the charges will be taken seriously or because they can't afford the fees. However, it is prudent to get legal help early on because a professional can advise you how to protect your rights and avoid making statements that can hurt your case. (For advice on finding a lawyer, see chapter 15.)

Contact Your Insurance Agent

Also contact your business liability insurance agent. Although your insurance policy will probably not provide legal help during a criminal investigation, your agent may be able to offer advice to protect you against a parent lawsuit. If a parent does sue you, your insurance policy will probably provide legal defense (see chapter 8).

Whether or not you have a lawyer, here are some recommendations to help protect yourself during an investigation.

- Start a file and document everything that you can about the alleged incident and the investigation. Write down your best memories of everything that happened. Keep a chronological record that summarizes your conversations with everyone you talk to— investigators, parents, outside advisors, and so on. Add copies of any previous records in your files about the child's behavior, parent conversations, medical forms, and so on.

- Try to stay calm throughout this process and not "blow up" at the investigators. Don't start making wild accusations of your own, or it will undermine your credibility.

- You can always refuse to talk to any investigator until you have contacted your attorney, or until your attorney can be present during the interview.

- Be assertive in asking questions about the investigation process, such as, "Who will you be talking to?" "Who made the accusation against me?" "How will I find out about the results of the investigation?" "What records can I see that are being collected as part of the investigation?" "Am I restricted from sharing information I have about this incident or this investigation?" "When will the investigation be over?" "Who should I contact if I have further questions or if I have more information to share?" Ask for a copy of the law and any written procedures that describe how the investigation will be handled.

- Be honest in all your dealings with investigators, and don't try to block their efforts. If you have concerns about how an investigator is treating you, contact that person's supervisor.

The Appeal Process

After the investigation is over, the various agencies will make their own decisions about what actions to take. The police may or may not bring criminal charges. If they do, you will need to hire a lawyer to defend you. If you can't afford one, a public defender will be assigned to you.

You will be notified in writing when the licensing agency determines whether child maltreatment occurred. If they find that it didn't occur, ask what information will be put in your licensing files and who will have access to it. Also ask what your licensor will say about this when a parent inquires about you. If you find that prospective parents will have access to records showing an accusation of child abuse was made against you, even if it was unfounded, you should write a note describing your side of the story, and have it put into your file.

If licensing decides to take a corrective action against you, and the penalty is minor (for example, they require you to take some child development training), you may not want to appeal it. But before giving up your right to appeal, find out if there will be any consequences for this negative action on your record. For example, if this penalty will count heavily against you in any subsequent complaint, you may want to appeal it. In addition, some providers who feel that they aren't guilty of anything may resent even minor punishment and want to appeal it to clear their name.

When licensing informs you of a corrective action they should also explain your rights to appeal the decision. Get a copy of the appeal process and pay special attention to responding to any deadlines that you have. If you are faced with a serious consequence, such as losing your license or having a member of your family disqualified from being around the children in your care, you should hire an attorney to represent you in the appeal. Usually the state licensing agency will rule on the appeal, and their decision will be final. Typically there will be no appeal to the state court system.

If You Are Sued

After all the investigations are over by the various government agencies there is still a possibility that the parent may sue you for money damages in court. Usually this won't happen until after the investigations are completed and maltreatment has been established. Although a parent can sue you even if the investigations determine that you didn't maltreat the child, they will be unlikely to prevail in court.

When a parent sues you, you are likely to learn about it when you receive the legal papers telling you to appear in court. However, before suing you, the parent may contact your business liability insurance carrier to see if it will pay a claim to settle the matter without going to court. If a parent sues you, you will need to have sufficient insurance coverage to successfully settle the claim without a lawsuit or to pay for your legal fees if it becomes necessary to go to court. (See chapter 8 for a discussion of business liability insurance.)

• •

State Abuse Investigation System Ruled Unconstitutional

In 2001, the Illinois state system of investigating and deciding cases of child abuse and neglect was ruled unconstitutional. It began with a case in which a parent who owed a family child care provider $800 accused the provider's ten-year-old daughter of sexual abuse because she had helped her mother dress some young boys. Although there was no basis for the case, the provider lost in the lower courts.

The provider's lawyers found that this was typical of the way other cases had been handled, and when they appealed the decision they filed a class-action lawsuit on behalf of all child care providers against the state. The judge found that the state had conducted one-sided investigations, failed to provide hearings within a reasonable time, and that their policies "harm the children of Illinois."

The provider's attorney believes that this case is not unusual, and that other states have similar problems with their child abuse investigation systems. If you have been accused of child abuse, this case may help you make an argument that your state's investigation system is fundamentally flawed. For more information, contact the law offices of Lehrer and Redleaf in Chicago at 312-332-2121 or lehred1@aol.com.

• •

Suing Your Accuser

If you have been falsely accused of child abuse, you may be tempted to sue your accuser. However, it can be very difficult to do this successfully. Your state law may make it impossible to discover your accuser's name, and you will probably have trouble proving that the person made the accusation knowing that it was false. It will be difficult to succeed without independent witnesses who can testify to this. The best course of action is to consult a lawyer who will be able to advise you of your chances.

CHAPTER FIVE

Travel and Transportation

Chapter Summary
This chapter discusses how to manage the business risks that are associated with
transporting and traveling with the children in your care.

Whenever you transport or travel with the children in your care, you expose them (and
yourself) to additional risks that aren't as easy to identify or manage as the risks in your
home. In addition, you may be liable for the children's safety and behavior not only while
they're in your care, but also after they leave your program, until they reach their next
destination.

When it comes to transportation issues, there are three basic guidelines that you should
follow in any questionable situation:

- Ask your licensor about your state regulations—What are you required to do? What are
  you not allowed to do?
- Make sure that your business liability insurance covers all the decisions that you make.
  Don't make any decision that will leave you uninsured.
- If you're uncomfortable with a situation, don't allow it.

In addition to following these general guidelines, you need to understand the issues involved
in two specific areas—taking the children in your care on field trips and your responsibilities
for children who are traveling to and from your program.

Field Trips

Accidents are more likely to happen when the children in your care are traveling or visiting
a strange place. Therefore, it's important to have a field trip policy that requires parents to
sign a permission form whenever you travel outside your home with the children. Most family child care providers include a general field trip permission form in their contract.
Although this can serve for routine travel, for special field trips or events, you should get a
specific permission form signed by each parent. (See appendix A for a sample form.)

Getting a signed permission form will not absolve you of the risks involved in traveling with the children. Even if your permission form includes a statement that you are assuming no liability if a child is injured, this disclaimer probably won't hold up in court. The purpose of the permission form is to inform the parents and ask them to share some of the risk by making a decision whether to allow the child to take the trip. If a parent doesn't know that her child is on the field trip, and the child is injured, the parent will be more likely to sue you. If a parent doesn't want you to take her child on a specific field trip, you must abide by that decision.

After the Children Leave Your Home

In general, parents are responsible for their children until they drop them off on your property. So if a child is injured in a car accident on the way to your program, you are not liable. In addition, if a child is injured while coming to your home from school, you are also probably not liable, because the child is not under your supervision until he or she reaches your property.

If a child leaves your property to walk to school, home, or the bus stop, you can protect yourself by following these steps:

- Ask your licensor if it is safe for the child to leave your home without adult supervision Also, find out if allowing the child to leave unsupervised will create a situation where you, as a mandated reporter, must report to child protection. If your licensor doesn't approve, do not allow the child to leave your home unattended. You don't want to be in violation of any state licensing laws.
- If the child is accompanied by someone other than his or her parents, be sure you have the name(s) of the other authorized person(s) in your contract. This includes a child's older brother or sister.
- Get the parents' written permission allowing their child to leave your program without adult supervision. If the parents share custody (whether or not they are married), get both parents to sign the permission form. You want both parents to sign (even if they did not both sign the contract) because you don't want one parent to sue you later because he or she didn't know about the arrangement.
- Check with your business liability insurance agent to find out what, if any, protection you will get from your policy if a child is injured after having left your home.
- Make your own decision about whether or not you want to allow a child to leave your program without adult supervision. Even with the permission of your licensor and both parents, you may not feel comfortable with the arrangement. If this is the case, do not hesitate to refuse to agree to the parents' wishes. Insist on a different solution.

You may be faced with many different situations regarding the transportation of children from your home. One provider consulted us because a mother had notified her that she would be picking up her infant on a bicycle and riding two miles home. The provider was concerned that this was not safe for the child. We told her she could insist that the child be transported by car (the parent's car or the car of an authorized person) or by public transportation.

Waiting for a Bus

As school budgets get tighter, some schools are providing less transportation and reducing the number of stops. If a child leaving your program must wait at a bus stop, or is dropped off at a bus stop, that is some distance from your home, you may want to take some action to influence the situation.

You or the parent can call the school bus company and request a bus stop in front of your home. If possible, make this request before the school year begins; once the bus route is set for the year, it may be difficult to change. Some school bus drivers will be sympathetic to your request; they also face liability issues in working with children. If the bus company won't agree to add a stop, ask the school for help in changing the pickup location.

If you can see the bus stop from your home, ask your licensor whether state law allows you to let a child go to, or return from, a bus stop alone. If you can't see the bus stop from your home, you may want to wait at the bus stop (if possible) until the child gets on the bus.

Discuss the situation with the child's parents. If you both agree that the child can wait at the bus stop alone, require the parents to sign a permission slip that specifies how far the bus stop is from your home.

• •

An Empty House?

Here's a travel dilemma that one provider faced. A child's mother was injured, and the mother asked the provider to let her child walk to and from the provider's home while she was recuperating. The provider's licensor approved the arrangement, and at first, it worked fine. However, the provider became concerned when the child began arriving late and at a different time every morning.

The mother would call the provider every morning and afternoon to tell her that she was home. But the provider noticed that although the mother regularly called from her home phone in the mornings, she always called from a cell phone in the afternoon. The provider became concerned that the mother wasn't really calling from home in the afternoon. And the provider could be held responsible if she was sending the child home to an empty house.

In the end, the provider decided that she would no longer allow this arrangement, despite her licensor's approval. It's always best to follow your own instincts.

• •

Enforcing Your Pickup Policy

Your contract should include a pickup policy that ensures the safety of the children in your care. Most family child care providers ask parents for a list of the people who are authorized to pick up a child. This should be a written list that includes each person's full name, address, work and home phone numbers, and e-mail address. You need to ensure that everyone who works in your business—whether employee or unpaid helper—understands and follows these procedures.

Don't let a child leave with anyone whom you're not certain is authorized to pick up that child. This means that you need to be able to confirm that anyone who shows up claiming to be on the authorized list is in fact that person. If an unknown person arrives at your home, at minimum you need to ask for a photo ID. Even better, ask for a copy of the driver's license of everyone on the pickup list and attach it to the list for your records. Some providers even require that everyone on the authorized pickup list come to their home before they will be allowed to pick up a child, so that the provider can identify them.

Let's say that someone who isn't on the authorized list shows up to pick up a child. The child knows this person and seems to want to go with him. However, if this person isn't on the authorized list, you must take reasonable steps to prevent the child from leaving with him. Some providers will call the parent to get verbal authorization that this person can pick up the child. Others will refuse to allow a child to leave without written authorization.

You shouldn't try to physically prevent a child from being taken by an unauthorized person. However, do everything reasonable that you can to prevent the child from leaving. For example, you might stall by asking the unauthorized person to wait while you contact the parent. If the person won't cooperate with your efforts to reach the parent and insists on taking the child, write down the license plate of his car, and immediately call 911.

Although you're obligated to protect the child's safety, your responsibility doesn't extend to trying to physically stop someone from taking the child. If you act reasonably and someone insists on taking a child without your permission, it's highly unlikely that you'll be held responsible.

What if a stranger shows up claiming to be a child's parent? Perhaps when the father enrolled the child he told you that the mother lives in another state, is in jail, or is out of the country—and now a woman is at your front door claiming to be the mother. The first thing you should do is call the father. However, unless the father speaks with the stranger on your phone and confirms to you that she is in fact the child's mother, there is no way that you can confirm beyond doubt that she is the mother. In this case the best policy would be to refuse to allow the child to go with her. If she insists on taking the child, write down her license plate and call 911.

For information about what to do if someone shows up at your door asking to take a child and claiming to be a police officer, a government agent, or a child protection worker, see page 118. For information about what to do if a parent doesn't want the other parent to pick up their child, see page 116.

Parents Under the Influence

Your responsibility doesn't end with confirming that the pickup person is authorized to pick up the child. If you suspect that the person is under the influence of drugs or alcohol, you need to take steps to try to prevent the person from transporting the child.

If a parent shows up at pickup time impaired by alcohol or drugs, you probably have responsibility, in two ways. You could be in violation of your mandated reporting responsibility (see page 27) if the child is in danger and you fail to report it. You could also be held liable if the parent becomes involved in an accident. Talk to your child protection agency to find out if your state's mandated reporting law applies in this case.

In one case, a parent arrived to pick up her child and proclaimed, "I'm drunk!" to her child care provider. It's best to let parents know in advance how you will handle this kind of situation. We recommend that you adopt a formal policy that tells parents what steps you will take to protect children if you don't believe that they can safely transport the child (see sample policy in appendix A). Your policy should make it clear that you will take action to protect a child if you suspect that the parent has been drinking or is on drugs. You can call a backup person who has been previously identified by the parent to pick up the child, or you can call a cab. If the parent insists on taking the child, call 911.

Parents need to know that you will take steps if you have any reason to believe that a parent cannot safely transport the child. You don't have to give the parent a Breathalyzer test or require her to walk in a straight line. You can tell parents that the policy will be triggered if you smell alcohol on their breath. You must do all that you can to protect the children in your care, and most parents will appreciate your efforts.

• •

No Driver's License?

If you know that a parent doesn't have a current driver's license, ask the parent to make other arrangements for transporting her child to and from your program. If the parent refuses and leaves with the child, call the police.

• •

Make Sure that Children Are in Car Seats

You also need to ensure that the pickup person places the child in an appropriate car seat or seat belts, depending on the age of the child. Most states have strict laws that require parents to transport young children in car seats. Your state may also require that older children sit in the backseat rather than the front seat of a car. Ask your licensor about the laws that apply to you. You should get a copy of these laws and enforce them in your program as part of your transportation policy. Inform the parents that they are legally required to drop off and pick up their children in an approved car seat.

You aren't obligated to inspect each parent's car whenever a child is dropped off or picked up. If you can't see the car from your kitchen window when the parent arrives to pick up the child, you probably aren't liable. However, if you do see that a car seat isn't installed, you must act. If a parent refuses to cooperate and use car seats properly according to the law, you are better off terminating the parent rather than risk the possibility of a lawsuit.

If a parent comes to pick up a child without a car seat, ask the parent to go home and get the car seat, and then return to pick up the child—or offer to call someone else on the authorized pickup list who has a car seat. Another option is to call a cab, requesting a car seat for the appropriate age. Then send the parent and the child home in the cab. If the parent refuses all of these options and insists on taking the child, call 911. You shouldn't refuse to let the child go with the parent.

In a case like this, don't give the parent your car seat; you may be held liable if it's defective or if the parent doesn't buckle the child properly into the unfamiliar seat. Also, don't install your car seat in the parent's car yourself; you could be held liable if there's an accident and the car seat doesn't perform properly.

CHAPTER SIX

Sick and Injured Children

Chapter Summary
This chapter explains how to manage the issues that can arise in dealing with children who are sick or injured.

Although caring for children who are in good health always involves some risks, being responsible for children who are sick or injured carries much greater risks. A child may be ill when brought to your home, develop an illness during the day, or suffer an injury while in your care (either at your home or on a field trip) that requires medical attention.

As we have seen, a child's family child care provider will always be held to a higher standard than the child's parent. So you need to be prepared to handle these kinds of situations in a way that protects both the children and yourself. The first thing to understand is that you are not obligated to care for a child who is sick or injured (although there are special rules about caring for children with disabilities—see page 56).

In one case, an eighteen-month-old was having mouth surgery and the parents wanted to bring the child to her family child care provider immediately after the surgery. However, the provider was hesitant, fearing that there might be complications. If you don't feel comfortable taking on the responsibility for a sick child, don't let a parent talk you into doing so. As always, follow your own instincts.

Set your own policy about whether you will provide care for children who are sick or injured, and under what circumstances. If you do offer care in any of these situations, there are three areas in which you can take steps to reduce (although not eliminate) the risks associated with this choice: prevention, documentation, and insurance.

Prevention

Many states require family child care providers to take first aid and CPR training. But even if your state doesn't require them, safety-related workshops can reduce your risks and help you prevent injuries. You should require everyone who works in your program or regularly comes into contact with the children (your employees, volunteers, and the adults in your family) to attend first aid and CPR workshops.

Prepare a written emergency plan that describes how you will handle a fire, tornado, flood, or other emergency. Discuss your first aid treatment program and emergency plan with your licensor for her comments and approval. Discuss in advance with the parents how you will handle a situation in which a child becomes sick or injured while in your care. Give each parent a copy of your emergency plan, and have them sign a statement that they have received it.

Preventing Injuries

There are many ways in which a child in your care could be injured:

- Running and falling against furniture
- Falling off a swing set, teeter-totter, jungle gym, or other play equipment
- Playing with sticks, roughhousing, or breaking glass
- Falling while trying to get in or out of a high chair, bed, crib, playpen, or changing table
- Pinching fingers in a door
- Dog and cat bites that leave facial scars
- Falling down stairs
- Severe sunburn
- Slipping on ice
- Throwing toys at another child
- Being burned in a house fire
- Riding a bike, playing a ball game, swimming
- Choking on food
- Being hit by a car while crossing the street

With all these ways that a child could be injured while in your care, the most important things you can do to prevent injuries are to vigilantly supervise the children and maintain the safety of your home. Maintaining a safe home environment can substantially lower the chances that a child will become sick or injured in your care. It's important to conduct regular safety checks of your home, paying particular attention to the following:

- Locking up toxic materials
- Keeping dogs away from the children
- Maintaining the safety of the outside equipment and environment
- Regularly picking up your home to reduce the likelihood that children will trip and fall (or if they do fall, to reduce the seriousness of their injuries)

For more on home safety, see page 14, and ask your licensor, community health nurse, or fellow providers for other ideas about keeping your home as safe as possible for children.

Illness Policy

You should be sure to include an illness policy in your contract with parents. (For a sample illness policy, see *Family Child Care Contracts and Policies*.) Your illness policy should include the following stipulations:

- The parent must notify you if a child has or may have any one of an enclosed list of specified illnesses (ask your licensor what illnesses to list). The parent must make other arrangements for care until the child is well enough to return.

- You will notify the parent if the child is exposed to an illness or shows specific symptoms (ask your licensor what symptoms to list).

- You may refuse to accept a child for care if certain symptoms are present (ask your licensor what symptoms to list).

- If you believe that a child is too ill to remain in care, you will ask the parents to pick up the child as soon as possible.

- The parents agree to give their children all the immunizations required by law and notify you when each immunization is given.

- All the medical information that the parent provides to you will be kept confidential.

Immunization

One of the requirements in your sickness policy will be that parents should notify you of all immunizations. However, typically immunization is treated as a separate issue under state law, and often there is special set of requirements for this area. The biggest risk associated with immunization is that an increasing number of families are choosing not to immunize their children, usually because of religious beliefs or safety concerns.

Most states have laws that require immunization in child care, although some states allow exceptions to these requirements. Whether permitted or not, a child who isn't immunized places all the children in your care at greater risk. To protect yourself, you should give parents an immunization notice when they enroll in your program:

- Describe the importance and benefits of immunization. (Ask your licensor for this information.)
- Explain that parents who choose not to immunize their children need to understand the potential consequences of this decision, including contracting a disease, transmitting it to others, and being quarantined if there is an outbreak.
- State that there may be immunized, underimmunized, or nonimmunized children in your program, and because of confidentiality rules you will not be able to provide any information about the immunization status of the other children in your program.
- Inform parents that exposing their children to others who aren't immunized may increase their risk of contracting disease.

If you have concerns about caring for a child who isn't immunized, discuss this with your licensor. For more information, see "Unimmunized Children in Child Care Settings" published by the Child Care Law Center (see appendix B).

Documentation

You should keep thorough records of all the injuries or illnesses suffered by the children in your care, regardless of how minor they are and whether they occurred in your care. Maintain a logbook for each child, and in it record the progress of each illness or injury, detailing the medication and other treatment provided, and summarizing all your conversations with parents and medical professionals about the child's condition.

As described in chapter 4, you should report all injuries and illnesses to the parents and your licensor as soon as possible. In your logbook, record who you talked with and the date and time that you informed the parents.

Whenever a child in your care is ill or injured—whether it occurs in your care or the child arrives in that condition—you should ask the parents what kind of care they want you to provide. For example, you might ask, "Should I treat this injury with an ice pack?" or "What would you like me to do for your child today?" Record in your logbook all the parent's instructions to you and the actions that the parent asked you to take (or not take).

Keeping routine logbooks will be invaluable documentation if a parent ever decides to sue you. They can be used as part of your defense to show that you responded promptly and reasonably to an emergency by following the parent's instructions.

Insurance

When a child becomes sick or injured while in your care, who is responsible for the medical expenses? Unfortunately, there's no simple answer to this question. Some providers put a clause in their contract that the parent will be responsible. However, by itself this statement probably won't protect you from a parent making a claim against you. Some providers require parents to carry medical insurance for their own children, but there's no way to enforce this.

Parents may or may not expect you to carry adequate medical insurance to cover their children. Your business liability policy (or a separate medical expenses policy, see page 73) will provide some coverage for medical bills that involve accidents (see chapter 8). However, it may not cover a situation in which a child becomes ill or contracts an infectious illness while in your care. Whenever a serious illness or injury occurs, report it immediately to the insurance agent for your business liability policy and follow your agent's advice about how to handle the situation.

Handling Specific Situations

Although your ultimate goal is to protect the children, there are many different kinds of situations that can arise. Here are some suggestions for handling specific situations that involve sick or injured children. (For more information, see *Legal Aspects of Caring for Sick and Injured Children* by the Child Care Law Center; see appendix B.)

A Sick Child Is Brought to Your Home

Your state licensing regulations may specify certain conditions under which you may not accept children who are ill (for example, if a child has a contagious illness). In some cases you may be required by law to report a serious illness to your licensor.

Although your state laws may permit you to care for children who have a minor illness, such as a mild cold or the flu, that choice is up to you. You can either decide that the ill child would be better off cared for by her parents, or decide that you can handle it.

Some providers do a quick check of each child's physical condition upon arrival, and ask the parents to sign a statement describing any physical injuries or medical conditions. One reason for doing this is to help protect the provider from any false accusations of abuse. If you have any questions about the accepted health standards for children, contact your licensor, a community health nurse, or a local child care resource and referral agency.

A Child Becomes Ill While in Your Care

When a child becomes ill in your care, you must make sure that the child receives appropriate medical attention. Depending on the severity of the illness, this may mean giving the child medications, providing a separate room for the child to lie down in, or calling 911 or an ambulance.

Some states allow you to give a child a one-time dose of a medication if you get verbal permission from the parent by phone. Other states won't allow you to give any medications without written permission from the parent. If your state requires written permission, it isn't enough to include this in your contract; you will need specific written permission for every situation that arises. Ask your licensor for the rules in your state (see page 56 for more information on medications).

Whenever a child gets sick, call the child's parents right away. You can either ask the parent to pick up the child immediately, or you can ask the parent how to care for the child at your home for the day. If a child has a contagious disease, separate the child from the other children in your care, and notify the other parents to watch out for symptoms of the illness. Ask your licensor what criteria you should use to determine if a child should be separated from the others. For example, do you need to isolate a child who has a common cold?

A Child Becomes Injured While in Your Care

Any unexplained injury could lead to a complaint against you. When a child is injured in your care, you should always promptly call the child's parent, report the injury to your licensor, and record all conversations about the injury in your logbook. However, your first steps should always be to provide first aid or seek emergency treatment for the child, and then call the parent and your licensor. How you should respond to an injury will depend primarily on its severity and whether the child requires immediate medical attention:

- If the injury is quite minor (like a bump on the head), and the child seems fine, simply follow the basic requirements to contact the parents and your licensor and record the injury in your logbook.

- If the injury is relatively minor and doesn't require immediate attention (the child is alert and any bleeding is under control), contact the parents and ask them to assume responsibility for the child's medical care.

- If the injury is more serious, and the child needs immediate attention, ask the parents to pick up the child. If this isn't possible, ask the parents what they want you to do (take the child to a hospital or clinic, call another person to take the child, and so on).

- If the injury is major, call 911 immediately.

Planning ahead will help you reduce the consequences of injuries to the children in your care. Prepare an emergency plan for how you will assist injured children. Ask the parents and your licensor to review the plan and give you feedback. Your emergency planning should include the following:

- Keep updated parent phone numbers and emergency service numbers by your telephone.

- Arrange for emergency backup supervision for the other children in your care in case you have to drive an injured child to a clinic or the emergency room.

- Memorize the quickest route to the nearest hospital.

A Child Becomes Sick or Injured on a Field Trip

Anytime you take the children out of your home you should always bring a first-aid kit, the phone numbers for all the children's parents and doctors, and signed authorizations from all the parents for emergency medical treatment. If a child is injured or falls ill, get immediate medical help and notify the parents and your licensor.

It's important to get signed permission forms from parents whenever you take the children out of your home. If a trip is a regular outing (such as a daily trip to the park) then it's sufficient to have the parents sign a general field trip permission form when they enroll the child. However, for special field trips, you should get signed permission forms each time (see page 43). Here are more suggestions for keeping children safe on field trips:

- As mentioned above, always bring a first-aid kit, the phone numbers for all the children's parents and doctors, and signed authorizations from all the parents for emergency medical treatment.

- You may want to take another adult along to provide the additional supervision that may be needed in a strange environment.

- Develop safety rules for the children to follow and rehearse them regularly.

- Review your business liability insurance policy to make sure that it will cover injuries suffered by children on trips away from your home (see chapter 8).

- If you transport the children in a vehicle, make sure that your vehicle insurance will protect you if a child is injured in your vehicle and the parent sues you (see chapter 9).

A Child Needs Medication While in Your Care

Your state regulations may specify under what circumstances you are allowed to administer medication to a sick child, and you should always follow those rules. If this is permitted, you usually have a great deal of leeway in deciding whether to administer any medications (there is an exception for children who have a disability; see box at the end of this section).

If you choose to administer any prescription or nonprescription medication (including aspirin), you should first get written permission signed by both parents and the child's doctor. This document should include the following:

- The date
- The name of the medication
- The dosage
- The times and dates that the medication is to be given
- The period of time over which the medication is to be given
- The prescribing physician's name and phone number
- Any additional information about possible side effects, whether to give the medication with food, storage instructions, or other instructions

If the parent refuses to sign the permission form, don't give the child any medication. Whenever you administer medication to a child, take the following precautions:

- Make sure that the medication is in the original container and that it was prescribed for that child. (Parents may ask you to administer medicine that was originally prescribed to a sibling for the same illness.)
- Clearly label the medication container with the child's name.
- Administer the medication only in the dosage and at the times indicated.
- Store the medication as directed (refrigerated if necessary) and out of reach of children.
- Record in your log book what medications you gave to the child, how much, and when.
- Communicate all this information to the parents.
- Return any unused medication to the parent. Throw it away after the expiration date passes or the family withdraws from your program.

What should you do if you know that a child's doctor has prescribed medication (such as Ritalin, for example) for a child, and the child's parent refuses to give the drug to the child? You should never administer medications to a child without the parent's permission. If, in your opinion, the child is not receiving adequate care because the parent isn't administering prescribed medications, do your best to convince the parent to follow the doctor's advice or ask the parent to seek out a second medical opinion.

If you're concerned about a child's health or the safety of the other children in your care, and you're unable to get the parent's cooperation, call your child protection agency and ask their advice about whether you have a mandated responsibility to report the parent, as described on page 27.

ADA and Medications

Although you may prefer not to administer medications at all, the Americans with Disabilities Act requires you to do so for children who have certain chronic conditions, such as asthma, if doing so would enable the child to participate in your program (see chapter 13).

According to the ADA, you can't be required to administer a medication if it requires a special skill that you can only obtain with significant difficulty or expense. However, the field of medicine changes rapidly, and each state sets its own standards, so the rules that require you to give shots or assist with inhaled medication could change. Ask your licensor about your responsibilities in your state.

You may discover that the federal ADA regulations are in conflict with your state law when it comes to dispensing medications. In some cases, the ADA will overrule the state law. If you face this situation, ask your licensor for guidance. If your licensor tells you not to dispense medications, tell the parents that you can't do it. If the parents say that they will file a complaint against you for this, tell them to go ahead in order to clarify your responsibilities under the law.

A Child Needs Immediate Medical Attention While in Your Care

When a child in your care needs immediate medical attention, you should first contact the hospital or rescue squad, and then the child's parents and your licensor. If you ever face this kind of situation, it will be essential to be well prepared. Here are some steps that you should take in advance:

- Get a medical treatment authorization form for every child, signed by both parents who have legal custody. Put the forms in a safe, easily accessible place. Give a copy of the signed forms to each child's doctor.

- Go to the hospital nearest your home and ask what procedures they follow when a non-relative brings a child in for emergency treatment. Most hospitals will provide treatment if you have a medical treatment authorization form. However, some hospitals may require parents to sign their own form, or they may require telephone confirmation from a parent or the child's insurance information. If the hospital has its own medical treatment authorization form, require both parents to sign it and make sure that these forms are on file at the hospital.

- Contact your local rescue squad and ask what information (such as health insurance policy or Social Security number) they would need in an emergency. Get this information from all parents and keep it with each child's medical treatment authorization form.

Sudden Infant Death Syndrome

Sudden Infant Death Syndrome (SIDS) is a condition in which otherwise healthy infants die suddenly, usually during sleep. In this country about 3,000 babies die of SIDS each year, and about 20% of these deaths occur in child care centers and family child care programs. Most SIDS deaths in family child care settings occur within the first week of care, usually in the first day or two.

Although the cause of SIDS is unknown, you can reduce its risks by making it a policy to always follow these simple procedures:

- Make sure that all infants under age one sleep only on their backs on a firm surface. (Back sleeping is the most important way to reduce the risk of SIDS and the most important precaution that you can take.)
- Don't put any thick comforters, stuffed animals, or pillows in with a sleeping baby.
- Don't wrap a sleeping baby in lots of blankets or clothes.
- Keep a sleeping baby warm, but not too warm. Keep your house and the baby's room at a temperature that's comfortable for you.
- Make sure that your business liability insurance policy covers SIDS.
- Maintain a smoke-free environment in your home.
- Monitor sleeping infants; if an infant stops breathing, start CPR immediately, and call 911.
- Explain to parents the importance of the infant's sleeping position in preventing SIDS.

The American Academy of Pediatrics and the National Institutes of Health recommend back sleeping as the safest position for babies. Never agree to put a baby to sleep on his side or his stomach "just for a while," even if the parent asks you to do so because the baby is teething, has a cold, or prefers to sleep in that position.

If a parent insists that you put her child to sleep on its stomach, ask your licensor if you are allowed to follow that request. If you are, get a signed statement from the parent and the child's pediatrician. The pediatrician's letter should state that the decision to allow the child to sleep on its stomach is medically necessary. If the parent won't or can't obtain written permission from the child's pediatrician, you should refuse to provide care for the child.

In a 2001 case, a Connecticut jury found a family child care provider liable for a SIDS death and awarded the child's parents $800,000. The provider saw the baby sleeping on her stomach, but didn't try to awaken or reposition her. The judge ruled that the provider had a legal obligation to prevent infants in her care from sleeping on their stomachs.

Although this case isn't binding across the country, it highlights the importance of doing everything that you can to reduce the risk of SIDS. (Appendix B lists several resources that offer information about SIDS prevention and education.)

Insuring Your Business and Yourself Against Risks

CHAPTER SEVEN

Understanding Insurance

Chapter Summary
This chapter introduces the four major types of business insurance that every family child care provider should have, and the most important features that these policies should include.

This chapter explains the general principles involved in using insurance to protect yourself from major financial risks. As explained in chapter 1, you don't need insurance to protect yourself from minor risks. If you were to lose your contact lens, or your pet were to get sick, this wouldn't be a financially devastating event—and it isn't worthwhile to purchase insurance to manage those kinds of risks. (See pages 2–4 for an explanation of the five strategies for managing risk.)

Since you can't afford to insure yourself against every risk that you face, you should focus on protecting the things that will make a significant difference to the long-term well-being of your family and yourself. By entering into the family child care business you are exposing your family to serious new financial risks, and the best way to manage these new risks is through insurance.

Before you became a family child care provider you probably had insurance to protect you and your family against personal major risks. This insurance probably included the following:

- Health insurance to protect your family against serious accidents and illnesses
- Homeowners or renter's insurance to protect your home and your property
- Car insurance to protect your car and to cover the cost of any injuries to your family or other people in a car accident
- Life insurance to provide financial security to your family if you were to die

None of this personal insurance is designed to protect you against the new risks that you assume once you begin caring for children. As a business operator, you face a completely new set of risks that you must manage. These new risks include, but are not limited to the following:

Financial Damages

The risk that money damages will be awarded against you in a lawsuit. For example:

- A parent falsely accuses you of child abuse and sues you for a million dollars.
- A child breaks her arm in your program, and the parents sue you for negligent supervision because you left her alone for one minute.

Legal Expenses

The risk that you will have to pay legal expenses associated with a lawsuit. For example:

- A child is bitten by your cat, and fifteen years later the child sues you. Even if you win the lawsuit, you may have attorney's fees to pay.
- A parent falsely accuses your teenage son of abusing one of the children in your care, and you have to hire a lawyer to defend him in a lawsuit.

Medical Expenses

The risk that you will have to pay someone else's medical expenses. For example:

- A child gets food poisoning while in your care, and her parents incur a $3,000 emergency room bill.
- You're driving the children to the park when a drunken and uninsured driver hits your car. The medical bills for you and the children total $20,000.
- Your helper falls down your front stairs and injures her back.

Property Damage

The risk that there will be damage to property that you use in your business. For example:

- Your house is damaged in a fire, and all your business equipment is destroyed.
- You can't reopen your business for six weeks after the fire.
- During that time you incur $5,000 in hotel and restaurant bills.

• •

Consult Your Insurance Agent

This chapter is intended to introduce the most important general principles of insurance. However, the topic of insurance is complicated, and you shouldn't rely on this book for the final word. Insurance policies can change over time, and the rules governing insurance coverage vary from state to state. We urge you to talk with your insurance agent about your specific insurance needs.

• •

Your personal insurance doesn't protect you from the risks of running your business. Also, it doesn't matter how your business is structured—you will still need to buy the same business insurance to protect yourself and your family whether your business is a sole proprietorship, a partnership, a limited liability company, or a corporation (see chapters 16 and 17).

Despite this, most family child care providers don't have any business insurance at all. When you think of all the disasters that can happen to the children in your care, and the large money settlements that juries have awarded, it's amazing that so many providers haven't tried to protect themselves against these risks. Statistics show that the average cost of a lawyer to defend you in one lawsuit is higher than paying the cost of business liability insurance premiums for 20 years. Once a problem occurs, it will be too late to buy insurance to cover it.

Many providers probably don't get adequate insurance because they don't think that they can afford it—but trying to save a few dollars this way could cost you much, much more down the road. (See chapter 11 for some ideas about how to pay for your insurance and contain your insurance costs.)

If you don't currently have any business insurance, this chapter can help you understand what types of insurance you should purchase. Most states don't require family child care providers to have business liability insurance, but some do, and some require providers without insurance to inform the parents, or have the parents sign an affidavit acknowledging that they know the provider is not covered. However, none of these steps would prevent you from being sued if an accident were to occur.

If you do have business insurance, use this chapter to review your current policies to see if they are adequate and appropriate for your needs. For example, although some states and branches of the military require family child care providers to purchase business liability insurance, the required coverage is usually very small. In this case, it may be a good idea to purchase more coverage than you are required to have.

• •

The Most Important Insurance Policy

With so much to think about in protecting yourself against the risks associated with your business, what's most important? Although it's true that you would suffer a setback if your property were damaged or destroyed, the most serious risk to you as a business owner is a lawsuit that finds you liable. You can replace your property and still stay in business, but it's extremely difficult to recover from a lawsuit that awards tens or hundreds of thousands of dollars in damages against you.

This means that the most important insurance you need to protect yourself and your business is an *adequate business liability policy*. This is true even if you care for only one child or are unregulated.

We cannot state too strongly how important it is for all family child care providers to have adequate business liability coverage.

• •

What Business Insurance Should You Have?

There are four major business insurance policies that most family child care providers need to have. Here's an introduction to each one, with the most important features that each policy should include. The next two chapters provide more information about each of these kinds of insurance, as well as some other kinds of insurance that apply in specific situations.

1. Business (or Commercial) Liability Insurance

This is the most important insurance policy that every family child care provider should have. It should include the following:

- General liability coverage for accidents and lawsuits against your business
- Professional liability coverage to protect yourself in case you fail to adequately supervise the children in your care
- Legal defense coverage, ideally with limits in excess of the general liability limits
- Child abuse—including sexual and physical abuse—coverage for you, your family, residents of your household, and your employees, with separate liability limits
- Medical ("primary") coverage that pays regardless of insurance coverage by the parent's medical insurance for medical expenses if a child were injured in your care
- Coverage for personal injury caused by you, residents of your household, your employees, and volunteers, for wrongful discharge, kidnapping, libel, slander, wrongful detention, invasion of privacy, and malicious prosecution
- Bodily injury coverage for food illnesses, dispensing medications, and allegations of corporal punishment
- Coverage for accidents when you are away from your home or on field trips with the children

We recommend that your business liability insurance company be an admitted carrier in your state and have an "A" rating for financial strength from the A.M. Best Company (see page 77). The company and the agent should understand your business and have experience insuring family child care programs. The policy should be an "occurrence" rather than a "claims made" type of policy (see page 76).

2. Business Property Insurance

This is the second most important policy that all family child care providers should have. Depending on the insurance company, this coverage may be either an endorsement on your homeowners insurance policy or a completely separate policy. In addition, some companies offer a "business owners insurance policy" that includes both business liability and business property coverage in one policy. However, regardless of the form they take, your policies should include the following:

- Coverage for the cost of all property used in your business (equipment, furniture, appliances, toys, and so on)

- Business interruption coverage for the loss of your business income if your business is shut down because of a fire, windstorm, burst pipes, and so on

3. Automobile Insurance

You will need this kind of policy if you ever use your car to transport the children in your care or if you use it for any other business purposes.

- Coverage for injuries and damages suffered in a car accident while your car (or another car used by your employee or unpaid helper) is being used for business purposes

4. Workers' Compensation Insurance

You may need this kind of insurance if you have paid workers (check with your state).

- Coverage for the medical expenses of any employee who suffers an injury while working for you

Business Liability Insurance or a Business Liability Endorsement on Your Homeowners Policy?

Although homeowners insurance is primarily intended to protect your home and its contents (see chapter 9), it also provides some coverage for *personal* liability and medical expenses. For example, it would protect you if your neighbor were to trip on your garden hose, or your child were to throw a ball through your neighbor's window. However, your homeowners insurance policy cannot protect you from the risks of running a business. Most homeowners insurance policies specifically exclude coverage for businesses operated out of the home, and often specifically exclude child care businesses.

If you would like to have more personal liability protection, you can purchase an umbrella insurance policy (see page 85) that will increase the liability limits of your home-owners or car insurance coverage. However, most umbrella insurance policies also exclude coverage for any injuries sustained in the course of running a business.

Some homeowners insurance companies offer a business liability endorsement (an amendment to the policy) for family child care providers. Many providers believe that they have adequate liability insurance if they have this endorsement. This is a major mistake. There is a big difference between business liability insurance and a homeowners liability endorsement.

Homeowners liability endorsements are very narrow in coverage, usually covering only a small amount of medical expenses and liability coverage, and you probably won't be able to purchase an umbrella policy to increase these limits. Although these amendments vary, they don't offer the broad coverage that all family child care providers need. Specifically, they usually exclude the essential coverage that you need for professional liability (see page 71), child abuse (see page 72), corporal punishment, dispensing medications, and accidents away from your home, among other areas.

In addition, these endorsements may limit the number of children in your care that are covered and may reduce some of the personal liability limits in your original homeowners policy. (In other words, these endorsements provide less coverage for any accidents that may happen outside of business hours when friends or neighbors come to your home.) If you have this kind of policy, compare its coverage with the features listed on page 78, and you will see how limited it is.

All family child care providers need a separate business liability insurance policy that provides broad coverage for major business risks. Although homeowners liability endorsements may seem like a good deal because they are cheaper, you get what you pay for. These policies are cheaper because they offer less coverage.

• •

What if You Are Providing Care in a Home You Don't Own?

Some family child care providers operate their business out of a home that's owned by their boyfriend or a relative. Regardless of who owns the home, if it's being used for a family child care business, the homeowner will need insurance for property damage as well as medical expenses and lawsuits associated with injuries to children. It doesn't matter whether the homeowner is charging you rent. Getting an umbrella policy (see page 85) won't protect the homeowner from these new risks.

To protect the homeowner from liability, you should list that person as an "additional insured" on your business liability insurance policy (see page 68). The homeowner should also check with his homeowners insurance policy to see if it will cover a home that is being used for a business. If it won't, he should seek coverage from another company.

If your boyfriend or relative rents the property in which you are doing business, you should make sure that they have proper renter's insurance to cover damage to the property (see page 83).

• •

CHAPTER EIGHT

Business Liability Insurance

Chapter Summary
This chapter will explain everything that you need to know to purchase business liability insurance to protect yourself and your family against the major liability risks associated with running a child care business.

The last chapter introduced the four major kinds of business insurance policies and explained why business liability insurance is the most important business insurance that you should have. In fact, we believe that no family child care provider should operate without adequate business liability insurance coverage. In this chapter, we will explain the issues and technical terms involved in purchasing business liability insurance, the major features to look for, and how much coverage you should buy.

● ●

Get the Best Available Policy
You should always comparison shop to get the most insurance coverage at the best price. Use the "Business Liability Insurance Checklist" at the end of this chapter (page 78) to compare the features of different policies. Bear in mind that insurance policies vary, and even the same policy may change over time or offer different coverage in different parts of the country.

What if you can't find a business liability insurance policy that offers all the features that we recommend in this chapter? In some states you may not be able to find everything that is listed here—in this case, the best policy may have most of the features that we recommend, but not all. If that's the case, compare the available policies and buy the best one that you can find. The most important features that you should make it a priority to get are child abuse coverage (both sexual and physical) and professional liability coverage.

● ●

Who Is Covered?

The first thing to look at in a business liability insurance policy is whom it will cover. For example, if you have an employee, and you notice that a policy your agent is suggesting won't cover employees, you should tell her to keep looking.

Your name will always be listed on the policy as the "named insured." However, there are several other people whom you will need to add to the policy as the "additional insured." You will need to list these people by name on the policy, and be sure to keep the list up to date. The list of "additional insured" should include the following people:

- Anyone who works in your business, including all employees, volunteers, unpaid helpers, and employees of Head Start who come to your home
- If your business is a partnership, list both partners
- All the members of your family and all other residents of your household
- Anyone who stays in your home for more than a few days while the children are present
- If you don't own the home that you are using for your business, list the person who owns that home (see section below)

Your policy may also include a separate list of those who are covered for child abuse. That list should include all your employees, all the residents of your home, and the members of your family.

If You Rent Your Home

In some states, if you rent the house or apartment where you do business you may be required to notify your landlord that you are doing child care, and your landlord may request to be listed as an "additional insured" on your business liability policy. In fact, in some states the landlord can require you to have a business liability policy if you are operating out of a rented house or apartment.

Listing your landlord as an "additional insured" is a good idea because your business does create extra risks for your landlord. For example, if a child is hurt in your apartment, the parents could sue the landlord as the property owner and you as the business owner.

Including your landlord as an "additional insured" extends your business liability coverage to your landlord. For example, if you have a policy with $1,000,000 in coverage per occurrence (see page 76), the landlord would be covered for any incidents that you are liable for. Although some business liability companies may charge an added fee for "additional insured" coverage, it's definitely worth the cost. It will help you maintain a good relationship with your landlord, which is always a good risk-reduction strategy.

Adding your landlord as an "additional insured" will not provide any property insurance coverage if your landlord's property is damaged or destroyed by a child in your care. In general, property damage caused by a child in your care will be covered by the parent's homeowners insurance policy. Any injuries that occur in a common area, such as the laundry room or parking lot, would be the responsibility of your landlord's insurance, because the landlord is responsible for the common areas on the property.

How Much Coverage Should You Buy?

If your state requires you to have business liability insurance, it will usually specify a minimum. In most parts of the country you can choose from business liability insurance policies that have coverage limits from a few hundred thousand dollars to a million dollars or more per occurrence. Your policy should have a separate limit for each occurrence and another limit for the total or aggregate amount. Policy limits are the maximum amount that an insurance company will pay for the policy term. The policy term is stated on the front of the policy and is usually for one year.

- The "occurrence limit" applies to each incident, no matter how many children are injured—if three children are injured in one incident, that is considered one occurrence.

- The "aggregate limit" is the maximum amount of coverage for all claims paid under that policy for the term of the policy (usually one year). Once the company pays this amount, the policy limits will be exhausted, and you will have no more coverage.

For example, if you have "$300,000/$600,000" coverage it means that you are covered for up to $300,000 per occurrence and up to $600,000 aggregate total for the policy period (usually one year). We believe that these liability limits are too low. However, no matter how high your limits are, as a rule the aggregate limits should be at least double the occurrence limits.

We recommend that you purchase as much business liability coverage as you can afford. If you can afford it, we currently (in 2004) recommend that you get $1,000,000 coverage per occurrence and $2,000,000 in the aggregate, or "$1,000,000/$2,000,000" coverage. Bear in mind that the limits that we recommend may increase in the years after this book is published. For the current coverage levels, ask your agent what upper limits are being sold now.

Buying a policy with limits that are lower than the recommended amounts exposes you to two potential risks:

First, if you have lower limits you may not have enough coverage for one serious accident or several smaller accidents in one year. For example, if you have an "occurrence limit" of $300,000 and you have an accident in which there is a claim of $400,000 against your policy, you may be forced to pay $100,000 out of your own pocket. If your policy has an "aggregate limit" of $600,000 and you have two different claims of $400,000 each, you may owe $200,000 out of your own pocket. You want enough coverage to prevent either of these situations from happening.

The second reason to avoid lower limits is that if you exceed the limits of your policy, it probably won't be renewed, and if this happens it will be very difficult to find new coverage. Any insurance that you are able to buy is likely to be much more expensive and offer much less coverage. This is a serious matter that could effectively put you out of business, since we don't believe that you should try to operate your business without adequate business liability insurance.

Should You Have a Deductible?

When you buy your personal car insurance or homeowners insurance policy, it makes sense to have a high deductible because it can significantly reduce your insurance premiums. In this case, you can put aside the money that you save into an emergency fund to cover the smaller claims yourself. However, when you're buying business liability insurance, this usually isn't advisable. As a rule, a higher deductible won't significantly reduce your premiums. Also, if you have to pay out several hundred dollars each time a claim is made against you, your overall costs will actually be much higher. In some cases, an insurance company may charge you the deductible amount toward the cost of defending you against a lawsuit, even if no claims were paid out. Although some business liability insurance policies may require you to have a deductible, for this type of insurance, the lower the deductible, the better.

• •

Get the Highest Limits that You Can Afford

A child in Montana fell off his child care provider's changing table onto his head and spent six months in the hospital before dying. His medical bills were over $500,000. However, the provider's policy had a per occurrence limit of $300,000, which meant that she had to pay over $200,000 herself.

No matter how careful you are, running a family child care business always exposes you to the risk of serious injuries to children that can result in chronic disability, long-term medical bills, and even death. This is why we strongly recommend that you get the highest liability limits that you can afford.

• •

What Is Covered?

Your business liability policy should cover you for a wide range of potential claims for bodily injury, including the following:

• Food illnesses (a child has an allergic reaction to a peanut butter sandwich)
• Dispensing medication (you give a child the wrong dosage)
• Allegations of corporal punishment (a parent accuses you of spanking a child)
• Injuries suffered when children are outside of your home or on field trips
• Actions of any paid employees and unpaid helpers in your program that cause injury to children

Your business liability insurance policy should also provide coverage for a wide range of potential claims for personal injury:

• Wrongful discharge (you let the wrong person pick up a child from your program)
• Kidnapping

- Libel or slander (you say something that damages the reputation of a parent or another provider)
- Wrongful detention (you refuse to allow a drunken parent to pick up a child)
- Invasion of privacy (you tell a prospective client that a child in your care has AIDS)
- Malicious prosecution (you accuse a parent of child abuse and the parent sues you for making a false allegation)

The other important areas that should be covered in a business liability policy include professional liability, legal defense, child abuse, and medical expenses.

Professional Liability

Professional liability insurance protects you against claims that you haven't supervised the children in your care properly. Let's say you fall asleep and a child wanders into the street and is injured—this will probably be considered negligent supervision, and your business liability insurance policy probably won't protect you unless it specifically includes professional liability coverage.

Professional liability insurance covers all the actions that you take as a professional who is responsible for the children. It should protect you in the following situations:

- A child injures or sexually abuses another child
- A child falls off a swing set in your yard
- A child suffers a severe sunburn
- A child is teased or tormented by another child
- A parent says that you didn't give a child adequate stimulation or allowed him to use inappropriate toys

In purchasing a business liability insurance policy, check to make sure that it includes professional liability coverage that will protect you against accusations that you failed to properly supervise the children in your care, whether or not you were at fault.

Legal Defense

Defending yourself in a lawsuit can be very expensive, and you want your insurance policy to pay for this cost. The key issue here is whether the coverage for legal defense is included in the general liability limits of your policy or whether it is "in excess of" these limits. You want the legal defense limits to be in addition to the general liability limits.

For example, let's say that you have a $500,000 occurrence limit, and an incident occurs that costs you $150,000 in legal fees. If your legal fees aren't in addition to the general limits, you will only have $350,000 left to settle the case or pay off any claims that are awarded against you. However, if the legal defense limits are in excess of the general liability limits, you will have $500,000 to pay any claim against you.

It's always best to try to settle before going to court—and the more money that you can offer the parents, the more room you will have to negotiate.

Bear in mind that legal defense coverage will only protect you if your policy covers the risk that you are being sued for. For example, if your policy doesn't provide coverage for child abuse claims that are made against you, it won't pay the cost of defending yourself against them either. If you don't have professional liability coverage and are sued for improperly supervising a child, you probably won't have any legal defense coverage. (This is another reason to get insurance that includes professional liability coverage.)

You want your business liability insurance policy to state that it has a "duty to defend"; this means that the insurance company will hire a lawyer and actively defend your case at their own expense. Occasionally a policy will say that it will merely reimburse you for your attorney's fees. In this case you will be responsible for finding a lawyer, and you may have trouble getting reimbursed for all of your expenses.

Your business liability insurance won't cover you when you're under criminal investigation. If you're investigated by the police or child protection for child abuse, you should probably consult an attorney, but these legal costs will usually not be covered by your business liability policy. Your legal defense coverage will only protect you when you are sued for child abuse and have to defend yourself in court.

In addition, you may find it difficult to find a policy that provides coverage for a lawyer to represent you at an administrative hearing to revoke your license. If you can't find such coverage, you will need to hire an attorney on your own.

Child Abuse Coverage

The child abuse coverage on your business liability insurance policy should provide liability protection and legal defense for any allegations of sexual misconduct and physical abuse. The important issue is to look for the definition of child abuse in the policy and who is covered by this protection. (See pages 33–41 for a discussion of how to prevent yourself from being accused of child abuse and what to do if an allegation of child abuse is made against you.)

The first question is the definition of child abuse. Your policy should include coverage for sexual, physical, and emotional abuse.

The next question is who is covered by the policy. If your teenage son is accused of abusing a child care child, or a child care child is accused of molesting another child in your care, the parents are likely to sue you as well as the accused person. So your policy should cover you, the residents of your household, the children in your program, and anyone who works in your business (employees or unpaid helpers). It's important to look closely at a policy to see whom it covers—some policies will only cover employees. In addition, your policy may require you to conduct criminal background checks on all employees or volunteers working with children. If this is not done, you may not be covered. Ask your insurance agent about such a requirement.

Because of the very high financial risks involved in a child abuse claim, the liability limits for your child abuse coverage should be separate from the overall policy limits. In other words, if you make a claim against your policy for a serious medical injury, you still want to have enough coverage left for any child abuse claim made during the policy term (usually one year).

As with general business liability insurance, you should buy as much child abuse coverage as you can and you should also try to get legal defense coverage in addition to the child abuse liability limits (see page 71). If your policy does not provide child abuse coverage for overnight care you will have to make a business decision if you want to provide such a service. We do not recommend providing care during times that you are not covered for child abuse.

It isn't possible to get insurance for a criminal act, such as sexually abusing a child or knowingly allowing a child to be abused by an employee or another child. If you are prosecuted by the state for child abuse, you will need to hire a criminal attorney to defend you at your own expense. However, if you are sued by the child's parents for damages in a civil lawsuit, you will want to have an insurance policy that will pay for your legal defense.

Medical Expenses

Medical injury expenses are the most common type of claim made against business liability insurance policies (the most common injuries are caused by tripping and falling). Your business liability policy should cover the medical expenses for injuries to the children in your care and their parents, including necessary medical, surgical, and dental expenses for accidents to child care children and their parents around your home. A typical business liability policy will have about $5,000 of accidental medical expense coverage. This is "no-fault" coverage that will automatically pay for any medical expenses that are associated with an accident in your business. If you can, find a policy that covers each occurrence without an aggregate limit. Although your homeowners insurance policy will also have some medical coverage, it won't cover any injuries that occur during your business hours.

It's best to get a policy that will be the "first payer" in the event of an accident. This means that your insurance company will pay the medical bills even if the child is also covered by a parent's medical insurance. If a child is accidentally hurt in your care, the parents will be upset, but if your insurance company steps in and takes care of the expenses immediately, it may help mollify them. In addition, the parent's insurance may have a high deductible that would require the parent to pay some of the costs. So quick action to take care of these expenses may make a big difference. The better your insurance company handles the situation, the less likely the parents will be to sue you.

Since medical injury claims are so common, this coverage is important. If you wish, you can buy a separate medical expenses insurance policy that will provide higher limits (up to $20,000) for more no-fault coverage. One advantage of this is that you can make your medical claims against the separate policy, rather than your business liability policy. (Minimizing the claims against your business liability policy can help keep your premiums from rising as quickly.) The major disadvantage is that you may have to pay more for the two policies. Ask your insurance agent about the best way to get coverage for small and large medical claims, either through your business liability policy or a separate medical policy.

● ●

Medical Expenses for Your Own Children

The medical expenses coverage in your business liability insurance policy isn't intended to cover your own children (although some policies may offer some limited coverage). If your own child falls and is injured, your personal medical insurance will cover this. If a child in your care injures your child, you may want to seek medical reimbursement from the parent's homeowners insurance.

● ●

What Isn't Covered?

Every business liability policy will have a list of risks that it will not cover, called *exclusions*. These may include the risks associated with

- Water (swimming pools, wading pools, ponds, and so on)
- Trampolines
- Pets
- Mobile homes (If you have a mobile home, it may be harder to find insurance, and you should make sure that mobile homes aren't excluded in your policy.)

If you have exclusions such as these in your policy, you should seriously think about removing the risk. For example, you could give your pit bull to your grandmother, or sell your trampoline to the neighbors. Bear in mind that these items are being excluded from your policy because they're considered to be unacceptable risks by your insurance company. And if your insurance company is refusing to cover them, you can bet that the risk they pose is significant. Even if you think that your dog, trampoline, or swimming pool is harmless fun for the children, you may want to think twice before taking on risks that your insurance company is refusing to assume.

Some policies will reinstate the coverage for some of these exclusions if you pay an additional fee or if you agree to certain restrictions (such as a locked fence around the pool or the dog). However, because of the enormous damages awarded for injuries caused by swimming pools, trampolines, and dogs, and because of the high incidence of accidents when these factors are present in your home, we recommend that you eliminate them from your program if they aren't covered by your insurance.

● ●

Dogs

Dogs are dangerous, and dog injuries are one of the primary reasons that providers lose their insurance policies. Even one such injury can cost an insurance company tens of thousands of dollars. Some companies won't even issue you a policy if you have a dog, even if it's locked up. Most policies won't cover damages caused by certain breeds of dogs, such as pit bulls, Dobermans, Rottweilers, huskies, and

German shepherds. Some policies won't cover any injuries caused by a dog (or any other pet) and most state that dogs need to be separated from the children at all times. If you have a dog, be sure to follow your insurance company's guidelines about keeping the animal away from the children in your care.

If your policy excludes dogs, check if that exclusion is limited to dogs that are in your care, custody, or control. Otherwise, if your neighbor's dog were to bite a child in your care, you wouldn't be covered. You would just have to hope that the injury would be covered by your neighbor's homeowners policy.

• •

Legal Defense Exclusions

In addition to these common exclusions, your insurance policy will exclude criminal legal defense, and it is also likely to exclude legal defense during child abuse investigations and licensing revocation proceedings. Your insurance policy will not defend you if you are accused of an illegal activity, such as racial discrimination or refusing to care for a child who is HIV-positive (see page 133). Therefore, when writing your contract with parents, you should be careful not to include any language that could be interpreted as discriminating on the basis of race, color, gender, religion, disability, or national origin. (Your state may also have additional laws against discrimination based on marital status or sexual orientation. See chapter 13 for more information.)

Hours of Operation

Some business liability policies restrict coverage to "normal hours" of operation that are defined on the insurance application form. If you occasionally care for children after your normal hours in the evening or on weekends, be sure to inform your insurance agent and make sure that you are covered during this time. If the parent of a child in your care visits your home in the evening (with or without the child) this could be considered part of your business hours. Even if she's only there for a friendly visit, your insurance company might conclude that your personal relationship is based on your business relationship. It's best to err on the side of caution and get insurance to cover you in these situations.

If you provide care for 24 hours a day, it may be more difficult to find business liability coverage, particularly for child abuse claims. You should expect to pay more to be covered for extended hours of operation, since the longer your business is open, the greater the chance that an accident could happen.

• •

Read the Exclusions Carefully

As a rule, business liability insurance policies will cover all risks except those that are specifically excluded. So if you want to find out what your policy really covers, it's probably most revealing to look closely at what it excludes from coverage.

• •

Other Considerations

In addition to who is covered, what is covered, and what isn't covered, there are some other issues that you should be aware of in choosing a business liability insurance: "occurrence" vs. "claims made" policies, master program policies, and whether the company is an admitted carrier in your state and financially sound.

Occurrence vs. Claims Made Policies

A parent or a child can sue you for an injury many years after it occurred. (The time limit varies by state. It may be a year after the child reaches age 18, or a year after the injury is discovered.) To protect yourself against future claims, you should get a policy that has "occurrence" not "claims made" coverage.

A *claims made* policy will only cover you if the policy is in force when the claim is first made. However, an *occurrence* policy will cover any covered injury that occurred while the policy was in force, regardless of when the claim is first made. In other words, if you are sued 10 years after an injury occurred, the policy that was in effect at the time of the injury would cover you, even if you no longer have insurance or are no longer in business.

This means that long after you buy an *occurrence* policy, you need to be able to prove that you had business liability coverage and what coverage was in force at the time of the incident for which you are being sued. To ensure that you can do this, you should save a copy of all your business liability insurance policies for your lifetime and store these documents in a safe-deposit box.

Master Program Policies

A *master program policy* covers you as a member of a group chosen by the insurance company. The policy provides the same coverage for everyone in the group and it can be difficult or even impossible to negotiate any changes to it. There are differences between master policies; some are better than others. However, if you buy one, you will need to work harder to find out what you are really covered for.

When you buy a master program policy, you receive a summary certificate of insurance (which is usually just one page) and not the policy itself (which is usually dozens of pages). Without seeing the policy itself, you can't be sure exactly what is covered and what is excluded.

In addition, some master program policies don't provide separate limits for each provider who is insured under the policy. So if the other providers insured under your policy make claims that eat up the aggregate policy limits (the total coverage that is payable under the policy), you could discover that there's no money left to pay for your claim. On the other hand, since a master program covers so many other providers as well, it may be less likely that your policy won't be renewed if you make a large claim.

If you purchase insurance from a master program, plan to spend extra time talking to your insurance agent to make sure that you understand what you are buying. Because the specific language in a policy is critical in determining who and what will be covered, we recommend that you get as much information as possible before you buy this kind of policy.

Is the Company an Admitted Carrier?

An *admitted carrier* is an insurance company that is licensed or "admitted" to do business in a particular state and has met financial and other requirements set by that state's office of insurance. This includes setting aside enough money in each state so that if the company goes out of business, the state fund should be able to pay any claims that you make (usually up to $300,000). To find out if a company is an admitted carrier, ask your agent.

If your insurance company is a *non-admitted carrier,* that means that it is less closely supervised by your state. If a non-admitted company stops doing business in your state, you could have a problem filing a claim. In addition, the policies of non-admitted carriers usually provide less coverage.

Check the Company's Financial Strength

Since an insurance policy is only as secure as the insurance company behind it, you should check the financial strength of your insurance company—it should be rated at least "A" for "excellent" financial strength by the A.M. Best Company. The A.M. Best Company ratings are a widely accepted indicator of the financial stability and strength of insurance companies. (You can access these ratings on the Web at www.ambest.com. Click on "Ratings and Analysis.")

If You Aren't Licensed

Some family child care providers aren't legally required to be licensed, and some states have different licensing requirements for different categories of providers. For example, in Missouri providers who care for five to 10 children are required to have a license, while those who care for four or fewer children are legally exempt from the licensing regulations. However, insurance companies prefer to insure providers who meet their state's highest licensing or regulatory requirements.

Even if you are legally exempt from licensing regulations, business liability insurance companies will view you as a higher risk than a licensed provider. They may either charge you more than a licensed provider or not insure you at all unless you become licensed. If you're legally unlicensed and want business liability coverage, in some states your only option may be to get registered or licensed. Since unlicensed providers usually don't have similar problems obtaining homeowners insurance, you may be able to get some limited liability coverage through a homeowners endorsement (see page 65).

Many business liability policies will exclude coverage if your license or registration is revoked, suspended, or declined. If your license is suspended for six months and you continue to operate your business (even caring for one child) you run the risk that your insurance won't cover you in the event of an accident. In addition to the consequences of violating your state's licensing rules, you should also worry about what will happen if the child is injured and you have no insurance coverage to pay for it.

If you are an illegal provider (according to your state's rules) you will not be able to get business liability insurance and will have to assume all your business risks yourself.

Business Liability Insurance Checklist

Here's a checklist that you can use to compare the main features that we suggest you look for in a business liability insurance policy:

	Policy #1	Policy #2	Policy #3
1) Limits: occurrence up to $1 million, aggregate up to $3 million	Y_ N_	Y_ N_	Y_ N_
2) Professional liability coverage	Y_ N_	Y_ N_	Y_ N_
3) Legal defense limits in excess of general policy liability limits	Y_ N_	Y_ N_	Y_ N_
4) Child abuse coverage for all family members and employees	Y_ N_	Y_ N_	Y_ N_
5) Separate liability limits for child abuse coverage	Y_ N_	Y_ N_	Y_ N_
6) Accidental medical ("no fault") coverage	Y_ N_	Y_ N_	Y_ N_
7) Covers accidents to children away from your home	Y_ N_	Y_ N_	Y_ N_
8) You can list your landlord as an "additional insured"	Y_ N_	Y_ N_	Y_ N_
9) "Occurrence" form policy, not "claims made" policy	Y_ N_	Y_ N_	Y_ N_
10) Covers all the hours that children are present in your home	Y_ N_	Y_ N_	Y_ N_
11) Company is an admitted carrier in your state	Y_ N_	Y_ N_	Y_ N_
12) No deductibles	Y_ N_	Y_ N_	Y_ N_
13) Company has at least an "A" rating from A.M. Best Company	Y_ N_	Y_ N_	Y_ N_

CHAPTER NINE

Other Business Insurance

Chapter Summary
This chapter will explain what you need to know about purchasing business insurance to cover the risks of damage to your home or vehicle, interruption of your business, injuries to your employees, and other situations.

In addition to business liability insurance, you need to ensure that your business and personal property is protected against damage or destruction. If you use your vehicle for business purposes, hire employees, or face certain other kinds of situations, you will also need insurance to protect yourself against the risks associated with those aspects of your business.

Business Property Insurance

The first step in insuring your business property is to examine what is already covered under your homeowners or renter's insurance policy. Don't just assume that your business liability policy will cover your business property and your homeowners policy will cover your personal property—it isn't that simple. Although these policies may provide some coverage, in many cases it will be inadequate and you will need to purchase additional insurance. (If you are operating your business out of a different home, you will need adequate property insurance for both homes.)

• •

What Risks Are Covered?

Any property insurance policy will identify the specific risks that your property is protected against (fire, water damage, theft, and so on). If your property is destroyed, and the cause of the destruction isn't listed in the policy, you probably aren't covered. So if you're worried about a particular way in which your property might be damaged or destroyed, ask your insurance agent if you are specifically covered for it.

• •

Homeowners Insurance

The purpose of homeowners insurance is to manage the financial risk of destruction or damage to your home and any other structures on your property, such as a garage, fence, or shed. You should have enough coverage to rebuild these structures if necessary, and this means that you need to ensure that your coverage rises annually as inflation increases the value of your property. Note: If you are in the market to buy a home you should ask your current homeowners insurance agent to get a copy of the prospective new house's loss history report. This report will show any claims filed against the home in the last five years. You can then check to see if the damage was properly repaired. Previous claims against a home can affect the cost you will pay to insure the home in the future. You can also get copies of the loss history report from Choice Point (www.choicepoint.com) or A-Plus Report (www.iso.com; 800-709-8842).

If your home were destroyed, you would lose not only the house itself but also everything that it contains. Your homeowners insurance will also protect the contents of your home, such as your furniture, appliances, jewelry, and clothing. A typical homeowners policy will cover the value of your personal property up to 70% of the value of your home. So if your home is valued at $100,000, you will typically have $70,000 of protection for your furniture, appliances, clothing, and so on.

Is Your Business Property Covered?

Once you open a child care business in your home, your homeowners policy may no longer provide you with that kind of complete coverage for the contents of your home. Usually it will not cover any business property, except for a small amount, perhaps $1,000 to $5,000. However, the critical question is exactly how the policy defines business property.

If your policy defines business property as the items that are used 100% for your business, then you should be able to easily identify these items (swing set, children's furniture, and so forth). If your 100% business property is worth more than your policy limit for business property, then you will need to get additional business property insurance to cover it. In other words, if your business property is worth $7,000 and your homeowners policy will only cover $2,000 in business property, you should buy $5,000 of additional coverage for your business property.

• •

If a Child Damages Your Property

If a child care child (or parent) damages your property—for example, if a child puts marbles in your dishwasher, destroying the motor—the parent's homeowners insurance should pay for this, rather than your business liability or homeowners policy.

• •

If your homeowners policy doesn't define business property as items that are used 100% for business, you are likely to have a problem. Some policies state that any items you have been depreciating in a business will be treated as business property. Other policies define business property as any property that has ever been used in a business.

Since most family child care providers use hundreds of common household items in their business and should be taking depreciation deductions for these items (see the *Family Child Care Record-Keeping Guide*), either of these definitions is likely to eliminate coverage for almost everything that you own. This might mean that your policy would no longer cover any household items—furniture, appliances, equipment, bedding, and pots and pans. Although the cost of each individual item might not be significant, the cost of replacing all of them could add up to tens of thousands of dollars.

In addition, many homeowners insurance policies won't cover any other structures on your property that have been used in your business, such as your fence, garage, shed, or playground equipment. If these structures were damaged or destroyed, you would get nothing from your insurance company.

Many family child care providers aren't aware of these limitations of their homeowners policy. A few years ago a Minnesota provider's home was completely destroyed by a tornado, and she lost all her household possessions. Her homeowners insurance policy replaced her home, but her business property coverage was limited to $2,000. As a result, she received only $2,000 for all her furniture, appliances, playground equipment, pots and pans, bedding, rugs, and so forth, since all these items had been used in her business. Subsequently, she went out of business.

Get the Coverage You Need

Finding out how your homeowners policy defines business property and how much it covers is the first step in getting the correct coverage. If you discover that your homeowners insurance policy only offers a few thousand dollars of coverage for your household items, figure out how much more insurance you'll need to protect all your property (ask your insurance agent how to determine this), and then buy the additional coverage. This may take the form of an endorsement on your homeowners policy or a separate policy for business property.

Some business liability policies also include property coverage; check your policy and see if this amount can be increased. As always, be sure to comparison shop—compare the coverage and the cost of all the options before making a decision.

Get It in Writing

It's essential to ask your insurance agent to show you how your homeowners policy defines business assets. Don't accept your agent's assurances that your property is covered unless you see the actual definition in the policy. If your agent can't show you the specific language in your policy that shows how you are covered, ask her to write you a letter indicating that all your property is covered, even though you are using it in your business. If the agent puts this in writing, then she will be responsible for covering this property, even if the insurance company won't.

We have heard from several providers who had pressed their agent on this point. Only after the agents did some investigating did they realize that the provider was right in suspecting that the policy only offered very limited coverage for business property.

If you don't have written assurance that all your property is covered—either in your policy or in a letter from your agent—you are taking a risk that you won't be paid if you make a claim.

• •

Business Property Insurance Is Essential

It's essential to properly insure your business property. To see why, let's say that a fire starts in your home that does $10,000 worth of damage. You haven't told your homeowners insurance agent that you're running a child care business—after all, she hasn't asked. Will your homeowners insurance cover your claim? If your business was the cause of the fire, probably not. In addition, the company could decide not to renew your policy because you didn't tell them that you were running a business out of your home.

Once you start a business in your home, you are exposed to great risks if you don't get the proper insurance to protect it. You shouldn't remain in business if you don't have adequate business liability insurance to protect yourself and adequate business property insurance to protect your home and possessions.

• •

What if You Can't Get Homeowners Insurance?

Some family child care providers are finding it difficult to get a homeowners insurance policy, and you may be concerned when you hear about another provider whose insurance policy isn't being renewed, especially if you have insurance from the same company. Because of this issue, some family child care providers wonder if they should tell their homeowners insurance agent that they have started doing child care in their home.

The insurance industry runs in cycles, and there are times when homeowners insurance companies won't renew policyholders who are family child care providers. This happens usually when these companies find themselves paying out large claims for business accidents.

What should you do if you fear that your policy may not be renewed? It's a mistake to do nothing. If you simply hope that you won't be discovered, you run the risk that there will be an accident and your insurance won't pay for it. If you have a homeowners insurance policy that doesn't cover the business activities in your home, you're taking a big chance. You must have insurance coverage for your home as well as for your business risks.

It may not be a good idea to speak directly with your homeowners insurance agent until you find out that whether your insurance company will insure providers. You may want to call a different insurance agent from the same company. In other words, if your homeowners insurance policy is with State Farm, and you're not sure if they will continue to cover you if they find out that you are a family child care provider, you could call another State Farm agent across town or in a neighboring city and ask, "I'm thinking about entering the family child care business, and if I do that I'm wondering if I'll be able to get a State Farm home-owners policy that will cover my home and personal property?" If the answer is yes, then you can contact your agent and discuss your new insurance needs.

If the answer is no, ask an independent insurance agent to search for a new policy on your behalf. If you still can't get a policy, contact the office of your state insurance commissioner to see if they have a program to help homeowners who can't find insurance on the open market (see page 102). If you aren't able to get insurance for your home while running your business, we recommend that you discontinue your business.

• •

Know Your Rights
Some states limit the right of an insurance company to cancel or deny you coverage for your business. For example, in Minnesota it's against the law for a car insurance company to cancel a policy just because the policyholder is a family child care provider. If you have questions about your state laws, check with your licensor, child care resource and referral agency, or state insurance commissioner's office.

• •

Renter's Insurance
If you rent your home, you won't need homeowners insurance. However, you'll still need to insure your business and personal property, since it won't be covered by your landlord's insurance. Your renter's insurance policy should also cover any fire, smoke, or explosion damage that you were legally liable for that damages the landlord's building. Check to make sure that it doesn't exclude any damages that are related to your business. A renter's insurance policy may also provide some personal liability protection for accidents that aren't related to your business. Ask your insurance agent how much coverage you should have.

Business Interruption Insurance
If there is damage to your home that requires months of major repairs, your business could be shut down for part or all of that time, and you will need business interruption insurance that will pay you for some of your lost income. Ask your insurance agent where you can get business interruption coverage. Usually you can get this insurance under your business property insurance policy or under your business liability insurance policy.

You will also need a place to stay, and you may have to live in a hotel and eat most of your meals in restaurants. You should make sure that these increased living expenses are covered by your homeowners policy as a personal expense.

Vehicle Insurance

Like your homeowners insurance policy, your vehicle insurance policy is designed to protect you against personal, rather than business, risks. However, using your car for business raises very significant risks, since one car accident has the potential to cause thousands of dollars of property damage, multiple injuries, and death—and none of this will be covered by your business liability insurance policy.

The first step is to find out whether your current vehicle insurance covers you when you use your car or truck in your business. Unfortunately, this isn't a simple question to answer. As a rule, you will be covered if you use your vehicle only incidentally for business, but if you use it on a regular basis you will not. However, each company will have its own definition of what constitutes occasional use, and you can't rely on what another provider says about her company. You need to get a written description of what your insurance company considers to be incidental and regular use under your policy.

Since the difference between incidental and regular use can mean the difference between full coverage and no coverage, to ensure that you have the proper insurance it's essential that you tell your insurance agent in writing exactly how you use your car for business purposes. Your explanation should include how often—once a week, once a month, or only in an emergency—you use your vehicle for the following:

- Transporting the child care children
- Driving to the bank to deposit the payments for your business
- Driving to garage sales or Wal-Mart to buy children's toys
- Driving to the store to shop for food for your business
- Any other way that you use your car for your business

If you don't tell your insurance agent all the ways that you are using your car for your business, the company may later say that you misrepresented your business use of the car, and raise your premiums, deny your claim, or not renew your policy.

If Your Business Use Is Covered

After you provide this description of your business use of your car, ask your insurance agent if your car insurance covers you or not. If she says that it does, the first step is to get this assurance in writing—in a letter from your agent or insurance company. After making sure that you are covered, you should take two more steps to protect yourself, especially if you ever transport child care children in your vehicle.

First, we recommend (as of 2004) that you increase the limits of your vehicle insurance coverage up to at least $250,000 per person and $500,000 per accident and your property damage coverage up to at least $100,000. You should have the same insurance coverage for underinsured and uninsured motorists. If your existing limits are lower, we recommend that you raise them to cover the extra risks of transporting children, even if you only do that occasionally.

Second, if you can't raise your limits to those levels, you could buy an umbrella liability policy for extra protection on your primary car or homeowners insurance policy. An *umbrella policy* provides added coverage that increases the limits on any given insurance policy. Umbrella insurance is relatively inexpensive, and you can buy it in amounts from $1,000,000 to $10,000,000. A one or two million dollar umbrella policy would be sufficient for most providers. You should get more if you have lots of personal assets or major risk factors, such as dogs, teenage drivers, swimming pools, trampolines, or renters.

An umbrella policy will usually cover only the risks that are specifically covered in the primary policy for which you are getting the umbrella policy. However, you should check to see if it contains any new exclusions. You can also get an umbrella policy to boost the coverage limits of your homeowners policy to increase your personal liability coverage, but you can't get one for your business liability or business property coverage.

To see how this works, let's say that your car insurance policy covers you for incidental business use and has a $300,000 limit, and you buy an umbrella policy that has a $1,000,000 limit. Your car is involved in a serious accident, while using the car in your business, that causes damages of $700,000. Normally, your car insurance policy would pay the first $300,000 and your umbrella policy would cover the remaining $400,000. However, if your car insurance policy did not cover you for your business use, then the purchase of umbrella insurance will not offer any additional coverage for accidents that occur while you were using your car in your business.

• •

Check with Your Insurance Agent

The rules for car insurance coverage can vary widely by state. Be sure to ask your car insurance agent for more information about the rules that apply to you.

• •

If Your Business Use Isn't Covered

After you describe your business use of your car, what if your insurance agent says that you aren't covered by your existing car insurance policy? If that happens, you have several options for how to proceed:

• You could look for another car insurance policy that would cover your business use.

• You could purchase a commercial insurance policy to cover your business use, although this may be very expensive.

• You could ask your insurance agent if there would be a way to reduce your business use to the point where it would be covered under your policy. For example, you might be covered if you only transport (or care for) a limited number of children at a time.

If none of these options work out, your last option is to stop transporting child care children. It's simply too risky to transport children in your car if you don't have insurance coverage.

Even if you're a terrific driver and you've never been in an accident, a freak accident could happen, or another driver could run into you. You can't eliminate these risks by having the parents sign a permission slip in which they promise not to sue you—it won't hold up in court.

If you can't get adequate insurance coverage, the only way to eliminate this risk is to stop transporting the children. Look for other alternatives, such as taking the bus, hiring a private transportation company, or limiting your trips to places you can walk to. You may also need to stop driving your car regularly to the bank or store for business purposes; ask your agent how much you need to cut down your business use to be covered by your policy, and get the answer in writing.

- - -

Never Charge for Transporting Children

Never charge parents to transport children (for example, $1 for each trip to school) or put a sign on your vehicle that includes your business name or phone number. Don't put any language in your contract that says you are charging for transportation. If you do any of these things, you may be required to purchase commercial car insurance and obtain a commercial driver's license (like a taxicab driver). Instead, simply increase your rates to include the cost of transporting the children.

- - -

If Someone Else Is Driving

If a parent offers to transport your child care children in her car, and gets into an accident, her car insurance should cover the damages and medical expenses. However, you could still have some liability because you allowed her to transport the children, and your business liability insurance isn't likely to cover the children when they are in someone else's car. Some business liability policies that have professional liability coverage may provide some protection in this situation.

Therefore, before you let anyone else transport the children you need to make sure that the driver is properly insured—ask to see her current car insurance card. You may also want to check her driving record. Although you can ask her about this, if she lies or forgets to tell you everything, you may still be responsible. The best approach is to ask her to give you a copy of her driving record and put it in your files. You should be able to get the driving record from your own car insurance agent, or you can obtain it online by searching under "Driver's License Reports." The fee for this service ranges from $20–50. Also have all the parents sign a permission form that allows their children to be transported by this driver and insist that the children always be seated in the proper safety restraints.

If your employee or unpaid helper uses her car in your business, you can buy "hired and non-owned liability" coverage that will protect you against lawsuits if this person is at fault and hurts someone else. This coverage won't protect your employee; if her vehicle is damaged, her own insurance should pay for the repairs.

If your employee or unpaid helper drives your car for your business, make sure that this situation is covered by your vehicle insurance policy.

Employees and Workers' Compensation Insurance

Many family child care providers pay others to help them care for children, either full-time or occasionally. In almost every case, state and federal regulations will consider these workers to be your employees, rather than independent contractors, no matter how little they work for you (see below). Hiring employees to help in your business raises two potentially major financial risks.

The first risk is that many providers fail to follow the tax reporting requirements for employees, which exposes them to serious consequences if they are audited by the IRS. (For more information, see the *Record-Keeping Guide* or the *Tax Workbook and Organizer*.) However, the possibility of having to pay back taxes, penalties, and interest to the IRS is actually a less significant financial gamble than the second, and more serious, risk—the potential liability if one of your workers is injured.

Before discussing how workers' compensation insurance can help you manage this second risk, we need to clearly understand who is considered to be an employee, and thus covered by the workers' compensation regulations.

• •

Other Kinds of Employee Risks

If one of your employees injures a child in your care, your business liability insurance policy should cover the child's medical expenses and any lawsuits against you. If one of your employees damages your property, you should be covered under your homeowners insurance or a separate property insurance policy. However, don't just assume you're covered; refer to the other sections of this book that describe business insurance, and make sure that you have adequate coverage.

• •

Who Is an Employee?

Many family child care providers simply call their workers independent contractors, and then ignore their responsibilities as an employer. However, you can't avoid your responsibilities simply by deciding that someone isn't an employee, and this is a mistake that can have very serious consequences. It is your state's definition of an employee—not your definition—that determines who is affected by your state's workers' compensation and state tax reporting requirements, and it is the IRS definition that determines who is affected by the federal tax reporting requirements, which include payroll taxes. (To learn how to fill out the federal tax forms required for an employee, see the *Family Child Care Tax Workbook and Organizer*. For information about your state tax responsibilities, contact your state department of revenue.)

According to the IRS, almost anyone you pay to help you care for children is your employee, not an independent contractor. Basically, a person is considered to be your employee if you have the right to direct and control the details and means of that person's work. There are three major factors that are used to clarify this—behavioral control, financial control, and the relationship of the parties. The more that these three factors apply, the more likely it is that a worker will be considered to be your employee:

- **Behavioral Control:** Training the worker and providing instructions for doing the work. If you tell a worker to follow your business rules, you are exercising behavioral control.

- **Financial Control:** Controlling the worker's ability to make a profit from her work. If the worker is paid by you rather than the parents, you are exercising financial control.

- **Relationship of the Parties:** Whether you have the right to control the worker. A contract that refers to the worker as an independent contractor is irrelevant if the relationship otherwise meets the requirements for an employer-employee relationship.

Based on the above factors, the IRS will almost always determine that anyone you pay to help you with the children in your care is your employee. It doesn't matter if the person only works a few hours a year for you. There are usually only two situations in which someone you pay may be an independent contractor:

- A person who comes into your home on specific occasions to perform specific services, such as cleaning your home, mowing your lawn, repairing your toys, or presenting a magic show or activities program.

- A person who is in the business of providing backup child care and represents herself as an independent business owner. To not be considered your employee, she should advertise her services to the public, work for several providers, work under a business name, register the name with the state, have an employer identification number, and work under a contract that she has written. This person should also purchase her own workers' compensation insurance policy.

In addition, if you occasionally send your child care children to another provider who acts as a backup caregiver, this person is an independent contractor, not your employee. This provider is not operating under your direction and control and is providing care out of her own home in her own business. (Make sure that the backup caregiver's own business liability insurance will cover the additional children in her care.)

● ●

Different Definitions of Employees

Bear in mind that different definitions of an employee may be used for your insurance policies, state regulations, and federal taxes. Your insurance policies may use the IRS definition of an employee (see above) or another definition written by your insurance company. The definition of an employee that is in effect for your state income taxes and workers' compensation insurance may be different from the IRS definition.

● ●

Workers' Compensation Insurance

Workers' compensation insurance covers the injuries and diseases suffered by employees who are injured while working. In most states, employers are usually required to purchase workers' compensation insurance. (In some states, such as Illinois, you are required to purchase workers' compensation insurance even if you hire your own family members. Contact your state workers' compensation agency to find out which regulations apply to you.) Some providers think that when they are paying state and federal unemployment taxes that this covers them for injuries suffered by their employees. This is not the case. Workers' compensation insurance and unemployment benefits are two totally different programs.

If an employee is injured and accepts benefits—such as medical bills, lost wages, rehabilitation expenses, disability income benefits, death benefits, and so on—under the state workers' compensation law, she generally can't sue you later for more expenses. If the employee doesn't accept these workers' compensation benefits and sues you instead, the workers' compensation insurance will provide your legal defense.

If an employee is injured, and you were required to purchase workers' compensation insurance but didn't, the employee may still be able to make a claim and receive benefits from the state. The state may then come after you for failing to purchase workers' compensation insurance. Many states have large fines (hundreds of dollars a day) for employers who fail to purchase this insurance, and you could also be held responsible for the employee's medical bills and lost wages. In addition, the state could shut down your business.

Many providers treat anyone they pay to help in their business as an independent contractor and are unaware of their responsibility to buy workers' compensation insurance. However, if one of your helpers is injured while working for you, she is likely to make a claim to the state workers' compensation department. The fact that you call her an independent contractor will not prevent the state from ruling that you were required to purchase workers' compensation insurance.

Your business liability insurance policy will not provide any coverage for injuries that are eligible to be covered under workers' compensation insurance. Therefore, if you have anyone working for you, it's critical to understand and comply with your state law regarding workers' compensation insurance.

● ●

State Laws Vary

Since the state laws about workers' compensation vary, this is only a general explanation of workers' compensation requirements. For more information, contact your
state workers' compensation agency or department of labor. In some cases, it may
also be advisable to contact a tax professional for more help.

● ●

Even if your state doesn't require you to purchase workers' compensation insurance for your
employees, it's a good idea to do so anyway, to reduce your business risks. If an employee
has a serious injury and then finds out that she isn't eligible for workers' compensation, she
may feel that she has no other choice but to sue you to recover her medical expenses. If your
business liability insurance policy won't cover you, workers' compensation insurance is the
best way to protect yourself. If you have any unpaid helpers who aren't covered by the state
requirements for workers' compensation insurance, compare what it would cost to cover
them through your business liability policy or workers' compensation insurance.

In some states you may also be able to purchase workers' compensation insurance for
yourself, either from the state or from a private company, even if you haven't hired any
employees. Depending on the cost, this might be a good option if you're having trouble getting medical or disability income insurance for yourself. However, bear in mind that this
would only cover you if you were injured while working. It would not cover you if you fell
off a ladder on Sunday.

Any volunteers who work in your program face their own risks, and those risks may be
passed on to you if those helpers don't have adequate insurance for themselves. Your business liability policy or separate medical payment insurance policy may pay for some of their
medical expenses, but probably little else. Also, if you have to file a claim for them, it will
have a negative impact on the cost of your insurance.

Ideally, all your volunteers should have their own workers' compensation insurance,
because this kind of policy covers far more than medical insurance alone. To get her own
workers' compensation insurance, a helper should first go to her car or homeowners insurance agent and try to get a private workers' compensation policy, since that's the least
expensive option. If she can't get private coverage that way, she can contact the state workers' compensation department and get insurance sponsored by the state.

Barter and Underground Workers

You still have legal and tax responsibilities as an employer even if you barter for child care help or pay your employees in cash:

- *Bartering* is providing child care in exchange for a service by the parent, such as fixing your car, doing your yard work, or helping in your child care business. These transactions should all be reported to the IRS as if money had changed hands. This means that if a parent is helping in your business in exchange for free child care, you need to treat this person like any other employee and follow all the federal and state laws regarding payroll taxes and workers' compensation insurance.

- If someone who works for you wants to be paid in cash, you may be tempted to avoid your tax responsibilities and make under-the-table payments to the worker. However, bear in mind that you run the risks of being audited by the IRS (or your state) and being sued if the worker is injured. (The employee also runs the risk of being audited or being injured without insurance coverage.)

Other Kinds of Business Insurance

This chapter and the previous one have explained the major kinds of business insurance that family child care providers need to protect themselves against the most common business risks. However, there are also a few other kinds of insurance that may apply in specific situations.

Covering Independent Contractors

If an independent contractor comes into your home to perform a service—such as cleaning, lawn maintenance, snow removal, or home repairs or improvement—you should always ask to see the person's certificate of insurance, even for a one-time visit. This certificate will tell you if the person is currently covered by workers' compensation and general liability insurance. It will also provide the contractor's name and address, so that you can follow up if the work isn't done well.

If the contractor doesn't have the proper insurance, you will have to rely on your homeowners policy for protection against any property damage. However, if the work is being done for your business, it may not be covered.

If an independent contractor is injured in your home, workers' compensation probably won't cover the injuries, although you may be able to get some coverage from your homeowners or business liability policy.

If an independent contractor injures a child care child, your business liability policy should provide coverage.

In all of these situations, it would be best for the independent contractor to have her own workers' compensation and liability insurance to make it less likely that a claim will be made against your insurance policy.

Family Child Care Associations

Family child care associations should buy general liability insurance to protect the association and its officers from lawsuits. An association could be sued if a provider or parent is injured while attending an association function—a monthly meeting, an annual conference, or the association's resource table at a mall. We recommend that associations purchase as much insurance as they can afford. Every family child care association should have a general liability policy, whether it is incorporated or not.

Family child care associations may also want to purchase "directors and officers" insurance; this type of policy protects against corporate fraud, financial mishandling, and negligence by the directors and officers. It also protects the association against bad advice given by the officers at meetings or trainings.

Association Meetings in Your Home

Many providers are members of family child care associations and hold monthly meetings or other association activities in their home. However, your business liability insurance won't cover you if there's an accident in your home during a meeting with other providers (either a formal association meeting or an informal networking session) because you aren't operating your business at the time.

Your homeowners policy should provide some medical accident protection and some personal liability protection. However, to ensure that you are covered against property loss and lawsuits, be sure to tell your homeowners agent that these meetings are occurring in your home, especially if any of the other providers bring young children to these gatherings. To increase your personal liability coverage on your homeowners policy, you can purchase an umbrella policy to extend your policy limits (see page 85).

Mentors

If you act as a mentor to other providers through a sponsoring organization (such as a family child care association or a child care resource and referral agency), the organization should carry insurance that will provide protection for you. If the association is sponsoring mentors and the mentors are in contact with the children in your care, the association should have insurance coverage for child abuse and professional liability protection.

If you mentor other providers without a sponsoring organization, your homeowners insurance may provide some personal property and liability protection, but your business liability insurance policy probably won't provide any protection. Again, be sure to tell your homeowners agent that you are engaged in these activities. She may advise you to purchase a separate liability policy to cover your activities as a mentor.

CHAPTER TEN

Personal Insurance

Chapter Summary
This chapter covers what you need to know about purchasing personal insurance, including health insurance, disability income insurance, life insurance, and long-term care insurance.

The most significant personal assets that you need to protect are your health, your home, your car, your earning ability, and your life. We've already discussed home and car insurance in chapter 9. This chapter will explain what you need to know about buying the following:

- Health insurance
- Disability income insurance
- Life insurance
- Long-term care insurance

Health Insurance
Nothing is more important than your health and the health of the other members of your family. Health insurance protects you and your family by insuring that you will get the medical attention you need. It also protects you from having to sell your other assets in order to pay your medical expenses. We all know that medical costs are sky-high and increasing every year. To take just one example, the treatment for a ruptured appendix currently (2004) ranges from $10,000 to $25,000.

Few people have enough money in their checking accounts to cover this kind of unexpected medical expense. To protect us against this kind of risk, we need health insurance to cover the catastrophic financial expenses that are associated with a serious accident or illness, such as a heart attack or cancer.

The primary feature that you need in a health insurance policy is coverage for major medical expenses, such as surgery, hospital stays, diagnostic tests, and so on. This is true whether you are insured through your spouse's employer or by individual insurance.

Many major medical plans are offered by a health maintenance organization (HMO) or a preferred provider organization (PPO). These organizations cover a large number of customers and use this to negotiate better rates with doctors and medical service providers. However, since these organizations only contract for services with certain medical providers, your choices are limited. You may not be able to see your usual doctor, or you may have to pay an additional charge for that privilege. If you're particular about which doctors you want to see, find out if your doctor is a covered provider for that plan before you enroll.

Your medical insurance should have high coverage limits to pay for catastrophic medical expenses and no (or very low) limits ($2,000,000 or more) for specific types of expenses, such as daily room charges or intensive care. You also want to be able to see a specialist without a referral. For tips on finding medical insurance, see page 102.

Disability Income Insurance

Disability income insurance pays some of your lost income if you are unable to work for an extended period because of a disability. Most providers wouldn't think of owning a home without homeowners insurance, or driving a car without car insurance. But the biggest asset that you have to protect is your ability to earn money to support your family.

If you are 35 years old and earn an annual net income of $20,000 for the next 30 years, you will have earned $600,000 by age 65. If you become disabled, your medical insurance will only pay your medical bills. So how will you pay for your family's monthly living expenses—mortgage, food, clothing, utilities, and so on?

Family child care is physically demanding work, and you must remain healthy in order to stay in business. One provider had to have hip replacement surgery and couldn't return to work for a full year. In the meantime her clients had found other child care arrangements, and she had to start building her business all over again. However, even if you are young and healthy, you could break an arm or a leg or become disabled in an automobile accident.

There are some ways to reduce your risk of becoming disabled. Learn how to lift children without straining your back (ask your doctor or chiropractor for tips). Get regular medical checkups, eat a healthy diet, and exercise regularly. At the start of each day, do a few stretching exercises to warm up your muscles. Try to keep yourself mentally fit by learning to relax and by taking short breaks during the day whenever you can.

Short-Term Disability Insurance

You can purchase both long-term and short-term disability insurance. Short-term insurance usually pays benefits after you have been disabled for longer than the elimination period that you have selected (usually 30 to 90 days) and will cover you for the benefit period that you have selected (usually 13 weeks to a year).

In other words, if you purchase a policy that has a 30-day elimination period and a benefit period of one year, and you have a major operation and can't work for six months, your short-term disability policy will pay you weekly benefits for six months, starting on the 31st day of your disability.

In most cases the scope of short-term disability insurance is too limited for us to recommend it. It will only pay benefits for a limited time, and this usually isn't a big enough risk to justify paying the cost of the insurance. Instead, plan to save money in an emergency fund or rely on friends and family to help you out if you are disabled for a short period of time. Also buy long-term disability income insurance, which will typically cover you after you have been disabled for at least 90 days.

Long-Term Disability Insurance

The two most important aspects of a long-term disability insurance policy are the definition of a disability and whether you can receive benefits if you are disabled for any occupation, or only for your occupation.

If a policy requires total disability, it means that you are unable to perform any work, not just child care work. If you hurt your back and aren't able to lift children, you might still be able to handle a desk job. If you suffer an illness that allows you to work only a few hours a day, you might be able to work part-time. In either case the insurance company might say that you aren't totally disabled and therefore can't make a claim.

Look for a policy that will pay disability benefits if you are unable to perform your own occupation, rather than only paying if you can't do any occupation. Also look for a policy that has partial or residual disability. This means that if you are disabled but still able to work a reduced workweek, you will still receive some disability benefits. You may need to add this to your policy and pay extra for it.

Disability Benefits

The long-term disability income benefits for which you are eligible will be based on your net income when you apply. If your income goes up significantly after that, ask how you can increase your coverage. Your net income is your profit after subtracting your business expenses from your business income. The net income of many family child care providers is low because they have so many business deductions. Let's say that you have $18,000 in revenue from parent fees and Food Program reimbursements. However, if your business expenses total $12,000, your net income would be only $6,000.

In addition, disability policies don't replace your total income—an incentive to return to work. Most of the policies that are available to family child care providers will only replace up to 50% of your net income. This means that in the above example, you would only receive a monthly benefit of $250 ($6,000 x 50% = $3,000 divided by 12 months = $250).

If your net profit is low, your disability benefits will be low. (Don't buy disability insurance if your net profit is zero, because it won't pay you any benefits.) In any case, you will want to compare the cost of the insurance with the potential benefits to see if it is worth it for you.

Benefit Period

The benefit period is the amount of time that the insurance company will make payments to replace your lost income (assuming that you remain disabled). The benefit period options usually range from two years to age 65 or lifetime. The longer you are covered, the more it will cost. If you buy a long-term disability policy when you're 30 and your benefit period is up to age 65, the insurance company might have to pay you a benefit for 35 years. It's best to buy the longest period that you can afford.

Exclusions

Most disability income policies won't cover preexisting conditions. Let's say that you were in a car accident many years ago and hurt your back; if that back injury still remains, it's likely that your disability insurance will exclude any back injuries from your policy. The insurance company will check your medical records, and if you "forget" to disclose a medical problem on the application, they'll find it.

Pregnancy isn't covered, since it isn't considered to be a disability (complications during a pregnancy may be covered). Also, any treatment for depression or alcohol abuse will nearly always result in denied coverage.

Life Insurance

Death is the one risk that you can't avoid, no matter how many adjustments you make to your lifestyle to maintain your health. However, you can minimize the financial impact of this risk on your family by buying life insurance. This insurance isn't designed to protect you; it's designed to help your loved ones after you're gone. There are two major types of life insurance—term life insurance and permanent life insurance.

Term Life Insurance

Term life insurance covers you for a specified number of years, typically ranging from one year to 30 years. The number of years you select determines the price of coverage. For example, a 30-year policy will be more expensive than a five-year policy, since you are covered for longer, and the chances of a person dying during a 30-year period are much greater than during a five-year period. Your gender, age, health, smoking, heredity, and the amount of your death benefit will also increase the cost of the insurance. Although it may not seem fair that you have to pay higher premiums because your father had a heart attack at age 49, that's the way it works. If your relatives suffered major illnesses at an early age, you may have to pay higher premiums.

Term life insurance is typically cheaper than permanent insurance. However, it does have some drawbacks. First, the cost of the insurance is only guaranteed through the term of the policy. For example, if you buy a 10-year term policy and at the end of the 10 years you decide that you want to renew the policy, your new premium is likely to be substantially higher.

Some term policies will allow you to apply for a somewhat lower premium if you can show that you are still healthy. However, if you've been diagnosed with any serious illnesses, such as high blood pressure, high cholesterol, or diabetes, you might only be able to renew the insurance at a much higher rate.

When you decide to buy life insurance, ask yourself how long you want to keep it in place. If you only need this coverage until your children get out of school, then the best option may be a term policy for that time period.

Watch out for term life insurance policies that start off with a low premium that increases after five or 10 years. Look instead for a policy that has a "level term" period in which the premiums stay the same for as long as you need that coverage.

Permanent Life Insurance

Permanent life insurance is very different from term insurance, and different companies give it different names, such as *variable, whole, universal,* and *cash-value* life insurance. The main advantage of permanent insurance is that it covers your entire life, and if your health deteriorates you will still be covered.

The cost of permanent life insurance is usually higher than the cost of term insurance, but it may offer many other benefits, such as these:

- A permanent life insurance policy has a cash value that increases over time, unlike a term insurance policy, which has no cash value.

- You may be able to borrow against the policy's cash value at a low interest rate. If you don't pay back the loan, the outstanding loan balance will simply be deducted from your death benefit.

- You may be able to stop paying the premiums and receive a reduced death benefit (this is called *paid-up insurance*).

- You may be able to convert the current cash value of the policy into monthly installments for a certain number of years or for your lifetime. (For example, you could pay medical expenses for a terminal illness.)

- Some policies allow you to add a feature (for an added fee) that allows you to waive the premiums if you become disabled. For example, if you become totally disabled for longer than six months from an accident or illness, any subsequent premiums would be waived as long as you remain totally disabled.

Should You Buy Term or Permanent Life Insurance?

Here's a summary of the relative advantages of the two types of life insurance:

Reasons to Buy Term Life Insurance
- Your insurance needs are temporary
- You need a large death benefit amount

- You can purchase it cheaply through your spouse's employer
- You would rather buy a cheaper policy and invest the money that you save

Reasons to Buy Permanent Life Insurance

- You have a permanent life insurance need (a family member with a disability)
- You need life insurance for estate planning
- You desire other tax-deferred investment options
- You may need to borrow from your policy
- You want to lock in the cost of insurance for your lifetime

● ●

Talk to Your Agent

Before you buy any life insurance, talk to a professional life insurance agent about the differences between term and permanent life insurance and which type of coverage would be best for you. Life insurance can be confusing, so take your time and ask questions. Your insurance agent should be able to clearly explain why the type of insurance she is recommending is best for you. Everyone's situation is unique, and you need to make sure to get the policy that will best fit your needs.

● ●

Naming a Beneficiary

When you buy a life insurance policy you will choose the beneficiary who will receive the benefit upon your death. Take some time to consider to whom you wish to leave this money If your children are below age 21, your spouse is the usual choice as the primary beneficiary, with your estate as the contingent beneficiary. (The contingent beneficiary receives the money if the primary beneficiary dies before you do.) If you are single or divorced, you can choose anyone you want as the beneficiary.

Be sure to name a relative or friend as the guardian of your children and your property in your will, in case your spouse doesn't survive you. Also, give clear directions in your will as to how you would like the money to be used (college, living expenses, and so on).

Discuss these arrangements with all the parties involved. If something were to happen to you, the last thing you would want is to have people arguing over who will take your children. However, it's an unfortunate fact that if you have life insurance money people may fight to get custody of your children.

Be sure to update the beneficiary of your life insurance policy if the circumstances in your life change—for example, if you are divorced or remarry. Once your children reach age 21, you should name them as contingent beneficiaries to ensure that your estate won't have to go through probate court. Also bear in mind that the insurance company will pay the beneficiaries who are named in your insurance policy, regardless of who is named as the guardian of your children in the will.

How Much Life Insurance Should You Buy?

Unfortunately, there's no magic formula to determine the perfect amount of life insurance that you should buy. Your goal is to buy enough insurance to meet your family's financial needs after you are gone. If you are married, have no children, both you and your husband work, and your husband can support himself if you die, then you may have little need for life insurance. However, you may need money for funeral expenses (typically about $10,000), uninsured medical expenses, and other unforeseen bills.

If you do need life insurance, look first at how much you are contributing to your family's income. You're probably contributing more than you realize. Besides your income, you may be caring for your own children, who would otherwise need child care, and this is a substantial cost savings to your family. If something were to happen to you while your children are young, your survivors would have to pay for child care. Many providers also perform many household tasks, such as laundry, cooking, cleaning, shopping, and so on. Your survivors might have to hire additional help to perform these tasks.

Next, look at your household expenses. If you were no longer around, some expenses might go up and some might go down. Your survivors might feel rich after selling your car and your snow village collection, only to discover that you have left quite a few unpaid expenses, in the form of medical bills, funeral expenses, and loans.

Here's an example of calculating your need for life insurance based on your financial contribution and your family's expenses. Let's say that you are making $30,000 per year and you have two small children. Your family has no other source of income. If you weren't around, your survivors would have to pay for child care, which might cost up to $5,000 per year for each child. So far, we have calculated that your family would need $40,000 a year to maintain their current lifestyle. To keep this example simple, let's ignore the cost of sending your children to college and assume that they'll support themselves after graduating from high school. That means that your family would need $40,000 a year for about 15 years. That adds up to $600,000 without taking into account inflation or the interest that this amount would earn.

Insurance agents can do more sophisticated calculations for you and tell you exactly how much insurance you might need to meet your needs. There are also Web sites, such as www.insure.com, that can help you calculate the death benefit you would need. To search for life insurance policies on the Internet, go to www.reliaquote.com or www.mostchoice.com.

Life insurance is particularly important if you have dependents—and many family child care providers are severely underinsured. Take the time to think about how an unexpected death would impact your family and calculate your family's life insurance needs. Fortunately, the cost of life insurance is modest compared to its benefits. A professional insurance agent can help you determine the kind and amount of insurance that would be best for your unique situation.

Long-Term Care Insurance

As people get older, the likelihood of suffering a debilitating injury or illness—such as a stroke, Parkinson's disease, cancer, or multiple sclerosis—increases dramatically. Your health insurance policy will cover the costs of skilled care for an injury or illness, but usually for only a limited period; these policies exclude coverage for long-term custodial care. Disability income insurance only covers lost income, not long-term care, and Medicaid will only cover you after you have liquidated all your other assets and become impoverished.

A long-term care insurance policy is designed to provide help if at some point you are unable to perform some of the activities of daily living—such as bathing, dressing, walking, eating, or toileting. Depending on the policy, this help might consist of paying for an in-home aide, a nursing home, or an assisted living facility.

All of these options are extremely expensive. The average cost of a year's stay in a nursing home is currently (2004) over $50,000 per year, and the average stay is two and a half years. Even part-time care in your home can be quite expensive. This kind of expense could wipe out your assets rather quickly.

Long-term care insurance premiums are lowest when you are young. It's best to get started in your forties, while the premiums are still low and you're still insurable. Although you will pay the premiums for more years, this will ensure that you have the coverage at the same low rate, even if you become uninsurable later.

Choosing a Long-Term Care Policy

If you've decided to protect your assets by buying a long-term care policy, plan to do some serious shopping around, since the coverage varies widely. Look for a policy from a reputable company. You may not use the policy for 30 years or more, and you want to be sure that the company will still be around then. Find out how the companies that you are considering are rated by Moody's (www.moodys.com) and A.M. Best (www.ambest.com), and choose one that ranks very high.

Make sure that the policy doesn't exclude mental illness, because this will often exclude treatment for Alzheimer's. Also, get a policy that will keep up with inflation, where the coverage rises with inflation. If your benefit doesn't keep up with the rising costs of nursing homes, you could end up owing the difference down the road. Be sure that the policy has lifetime coverage, not a limited number of years. Also, your policy should cover a home health aide, rather than just nursing home coverage. (Since the policy benefits for long-term care can vary by state, be sure to check for more specifics with your insurance agent.)

CHAPTER ELEVEN

Buying and Using Insurance

Chapter Summary
This chapter covers how to find insurance, how to pay for it, how to keep your insurance costs down, how to file a claim or cancel your insurance, and how to work with an insurance agent.

Since most family child care providers don't purchase insurance very often, it's not surprising that when they're ready to do so they often don't know where to look. One way to start is to search the insurance directory on our Web site (www.redleafinstitute.org). We have posted the names of some insurance companies that sell business liability, homeowners, vehicle, disability, and other types of insurance to family child care providers.

You can also get referrals to good insurance companies from other providers, tax professionals, your banker, licensor, Food Program representative, child care resource and referral agency, friends, and relatives. For workers' compensation insurance, your homeowners or car insurance agent may be able to sell you a policy. If not, she can refer you to someone who can. Many financial planners also sell long-term care insurance. Some other online insurance resources include the following:

- www.searchingforinsurance.com
- www.allquotesinsurance.com
- www.intelliquote.com

● ●

Talk with Your Agent
When buying a new kind of insurance, ask your current insurance agent if she can sell you the kind of policy you are looking for. As much as possible, try to buy all your insurance (homeowners, business liability, vehicle, long-term care) from one agent. You'll probably get a discount, and you're also likely to get better service.

● ●

Independent Agents

An independent insurance agent is someone who can sell insurance for many different insurance companies. Working with an independent agent can save you the trouble of contacting dozens of insurance companies on your own. Look for an agent who will check with many insurance companies that do business in your state, not just a few. If an agent tells you that he can't find insurance for you, talk to another independent agent who deals with different companies.

You want an agent you can trust, who will carefully select the proper coverage for you, and who will help educate you about insurance. It's worth your time to talk to several agents before you make a decision. Look for an agent who currently sells the type of insurance you are looking for to other family child care providers. Ask other providers for referrals to their agents, and ask for references before you select the one you want to work with.

Options for Finding Health Insurance

If you are looking for health insurance, start by checking out www.ehealthinsurance.com. This site is an insurance broker that lists nearly every health insurance policy available by state. After you enter in the specific information about your needs, it will give you a price comparison of all the available companies. In some cases you can purchase your insurance more cheaply online than directly from the insurance company.

If you cannot get health insurance at a reasonable cost, you may want to consider purchasing workers' compensation insurance (see page 89) for yourself. Although the coverage for your medical expenses is less under a workers' compensation policy, it is better than no coverage at all. The federal government offers a health insurance program, called Insure Kids Now!, that is designed to cover infants, children, and teens in families that don't have health insurance for their children. Each state has its own eligibility rules. For more information, call 877-KIDS-NOW, or go to www.insurekidsnow.gov.

If a health insurance company declines to insure you because you are high risk, keep looking; other insurance companies may be willing to take you. Some insurance companies will only take a limited number of people with a certain condition. For example, a company may only be willing to underwrite five hundred people who have diabetes. In this case, you may simply need to try another carrier.

If you or a family member has a serious health condition, it may make sense for you or your spouse to work for an employer who offers a medical insurance plan. Some family child care providers work a part-time job in addition to their child care business just for the medical insurance coverage.

As a last option, check with your state. Many states have insurance pools for people who can't get private insurance. This insurance will cost more, and the coverage will be limited, but it's better than nothing.

Options for Finding Homeowners Insurance

A growing number of homeowners insurance companies are refusing to insure family child care providers. If you're unable to find homeowners insurance, contact your state's office of insurance. Many states have programs (sometimes called the FAIR Plan) to help people who can't get homeowners insurance from a private company.

These programs are designed to be temporary coverage until you find private insurance. They should be your last resort for coverage because they are usually very expensive and the coverage is extremely limited (usually just for fire and weather). Most of these plans don't include coverage for your personal property or personal liability.

Paying for Insurance

It's one thing to understand that you need all the insurance policies discussed in this book, but it's another thing entirely to pay for them. The premiums for all these policies can add up to thousands of dollars a year. Some providers who are just starting their business put off purchasing business liability insurance until they have enough clients to afford this insurance. This isn't a good idea. Accidents and lawsuits can occur even if you have only one child in your care. It's important to protect yourself with adequate insurance from the first day of your business.

• •

Why Is Insurance So Expensive?

The rising cost of insurance is driven by many factors, including jury awards to victims, the stock market, terrorism, worldwide weather patterns, the discovery of new kinds of dangers (such as mold and asbestos), recent news of sexual abuse in the Catholic Church, and so on. Whenever insurance claims go up for any reason, the cost of insurance rises. Covering the risks associated with caring for children is affected by all these outside events, as well as higher damage awards in claims against family child care providers.

Some insurance companies have sold a lot of polices at a low price, been hit with a large number of claims, and then decided to stop selling insurance to family child care providers. This can cause other insurance companies to be more reluctant to sell to you. All of these factors drive up the cost of your insurance.

• •

After looking closely at the cost of business insurance policies, you may conclude that it's just too expensive to be properly covered and decide not to get any insurance. However, the cost of insurance is relative. For a few dollars a day you can buy a high-quality business liability insurance policy that will provide you with a million dollars of protection. Buying adequate insurance to protect yourself, your family, and your business and personal assets is simply part of the cost of doing business.

We have pointed out the most important features to look for in buying insurance, but getting the best protection does cost more, and not all providers will be able to afford it. In this case, it's always better to buy some insurance rather than none. If you can only afford to get business liability insurance with a $300,000 limit per occurrence, rather than the higher amount that we recommend, go ahead and get it. Don't leave yourself without any insurance coverage for your business risks.

Reasons for Not Buying Insurance

We have heard providers give many reasons for not buying insurance, but all of these arguments are seriously flawed.

"I don't have any money, so why should I get insurance?"

Many providers believe that they won't be sued because they have little money, but this isn't true. If a child is seriously injured, the parents probably won't be deterred by your financial situation, and if they do sue you, you'll have to pay legal fees. If the parents win a lot of money in court and you can't pay, they may be able to put a lien on your assets, depending on your state laws. In some states, they can garnish up to 50% of your or your spouse's wages.

You may be also required to sell your assets, although most states will leave you with some assets, such as a car, your house, and some money. For example, in Minnesota you are able to keep your clothing, one watch, household furniture and appliances up to $4,500 in value, the tools of trade for your business, your home, and a car up to $2,000 in value. The injured party can enforce the judgment for up to 10 years after it's made and can extend the judgment period for 10 more years if necessary. Other states will have different statutes; for the rules in your state, contact your state's attorney general's office.

If there is a lien on you, you may be required to take out a second mortgage on your home and it may be difficult to borrow money in the future. A lien can also make it extremely difficult to get car, homeowners, or business liability insurance. If you receive an inheritance, this asset may be used to pay the victims. If you get married, your new spouse may also be responsible for the judgment and your new spouse's wages may also be garnished. And if you file bankruptcy, the court may not vacate a negligence judgment against you.

So even if you think that you have nothing now, you don't want to be sued and possibly be responsible for paying a jury award for the rest of your life. A business liability policy can prevent this from happening for a comparatively affordable cost, perhaps a few hundred dollars a year.

"I've never had an accident."

Not having had an accident before is no guarantee that you won't have one tomorrow. Although you may never have had a car accident, or had your house burn down, you're probably insured for these possibilities, and the threat of a lawsuit can have much more serious financial consequences than the destruction of your car or home.

"I can't be sued for more than my coverage, so why buy any more insurance than the bare minimum?"
Not true. As described above, you can be sued for any amount, and if you lose the case you could be stuck with a lien on your home and your wages for many years to come.

"I have parents sign a contract that says I'm not liable if something happens to a child."
This won't help. The parents can't be prevented from suing you simply because they have signed a waiver.

How to Contain Your Insurance Costs
There are several strategies that you can use to keep the cost of your insurance policies under control.

Examine Your Existing Insurance Policies

- Talk to your insurance agent about what is covered by your insurance and what isn't. You may be either underinsured or overinsured. (For example, if you have both a business endorsement on your homeowners insurance and a separate business liability policy, you definitely don't need them both. In this case, get rid of the homeowners rider, because the coverage isn't nearly as good as a business liability policy—see page 65.)

- Find out what type of insurance (medical, life, long-term care) your spouse has through his employer and don't buy overlapping coverage.

- Before you hire an employee, find out what it will cost to buy workers' compensation insurance. If the cost is too high, you may want to reconsider hiring someone (unless your state law requires an assistant for the number of children in your care).

- Business liability policies are usually priced based on the number of children in your care. If the cost is higher than you want to pay, one option may be to reduce the number of children you are caring for.

- Some companies will allow you to pay the premiums in installments, usually monthly or semiannually. Take advantage of this option if it helps you better manage your finances.

Pass on the Cost to Parents

- Consider passing on part or all of the cost of your business liability insurance to the parents. To pass on the entire cost, divide the cost of your insurance by 52 weeks, divide the result by the number of children in your care, and then raise your weekly fee by this total. Here's an example: if your business liability insurance policy costs you $600 a year and you care for four children, you would only need to raise your rates by $3 a week ($600 ÷ 52 = $11.54 per week; $11.54 ÷ 4 = $2.88 per week per child) to cover the entire amount.

- Another way to pass on the cost is to add a surcharge onto your weekly bill each time your insurance bill comes due. You can remind the parents that they also benefit from your business liability policy because it pays for injuries to their children that they would otherwise have to pay themselves or claim under their own insurance policy.

Look for Discounts

Check with your insurance agent or company to see if you qualify for any discounts, such as the following:

- You can often get a nice discount if you buy multiple policies from the same company—for example, if you buy homeowners, car, and umbrella liability policies from the same company.

- Your homeowners insurance may give you a discount if you are a senior, if you install a security system or a smoke detector, or if no one smokes in your home.

- Your car insurance may give you a discount for insuring multiple cars, a good student, or a safe driving record. Keep your driving record clean; speeding tickets and accidents can cause your premiums to increase.

- When choosing a new car, research the cost of insurance before you buy; the more expensive the car, the more you'll pay for insurance. You may also be able to get a discount for purchasing a safer model.

- Long-term care insurance often gives a substantial discount to couples who purchase their policies together.

Keep Your Premiums Low

There are several things that you can do to try to keep your premiums as low as possible:

- Raise the deductibles on your car and homeowners policies. Increasing your deductibles from $250 to $500 can save you 10% to 15% on your premiums, and you could save up to 25% by increasing your deductible to $1,000. If you do increase your deductible, try to put some money aside in an emergency fund to cover any smaller claims yourself. (It isn't a good idea to raise the deductibles on your business liability insurance. In general, higher deductibles don't significantly reduce the cost of this kind of insurance, and you should look for a policy with no deductibles; see page 70.)

- If you can participate in a health insurance plan offered by your spouse's employer, it will be cheaper than buying insurance on your own.

- If you or your spouse recently left an employer where you participated in a medical insurance plan, you may be able to extend your coverage for 18 to 36 months with a COBRA plan. Although COBRA is often more expensive than purchasing a plan on your own, it may be the best option if a member of your family has a serious medical condition.

- Take care of your health. If you are purchasing health, life, or disability income insurance, your health will affect the cost of your premiums. The healthier you are, the cheaper your insurance will be. Although you may not be able to prevent some illnesses, there are many things that you can do to maintain good health. Exercise regularly, and eat a healthy diet to control your weight, blood pressure, and cholesterol levels.

- Don't smoke; smoking raises your health risks and significantly increases the cost of many insurance policies.

- Be careful with your credit. Many insurance companies will charge you more, or not insure you at all, if your credit is poor. If you have had past problems with your credit, check your credit rating annually, and make sure that it's accurate. There are three major companies that offer access to your credit report: Experian, Equifax, and TransUnion. See appendix B for contact information.

- If you have a lot of debt, make it a priority to reduce it. The insurance company sees that as a higher risk and will raise the cost of your insurance.

Set Up a Health Reimbursement Arrangement

Another way to control the cost of your insurance is to deduct it from your taxes, and you may be able to do this through a health reimbursement arrangement or HRA (formerly known as a medical reimbursement plan), which can save your family thousands of dollars in taxes each year. This is an option if you have family medical expenses that aren't covered by medical insurance and are able to hire your spouse or child to work in your business.

For example, Karen's spouse is also self-employed, and her family isn't covered by insurance. So she hires her husband to work part-time in her child care business, doing record keeping, yard work, and playing with the children. She treats him as an employee by paying him a regular wage and filing all the proper federal and state payroll forms, including state unemployment tax and workers' compensation insurance, if required. (See the *Family Child Care Tax Workbook and Organizer* for a detailed discussion of federal payroll forms.)

Now that her husband is her employee, Karen can offer him a health reimbursement family plan that will cover him and his family (Karen and their children). She can now deduct all the previously uninsured medical expenses covered by the new plan as a business expense.

The expenses that can be covered under an HRA include premiums for health insurance, term life insurance, and disability income insurance, as well as uninsured medical, dental and vision expenses, such as medical supplies, prescriptions, laboratory fees, hospital bills, orthodontia, hearing aids, eyeglasses, and contact lenses.

Setting up a family HRA for a spouse/employee allows you to cover the entire family, including yourself. If you hire your child and set up an HRA, the plan will only cover the child's medical expenses. Before you set up an HRA, you should seek the advice of a tax professional or a benefits company that sets up HRAs.

Deduct Your Insurance Costs

Many insurance policies are deductible in whole or in part on your tax return, and you should consider these tax advantages when buying the insurance. Depending on your tax bracket, you may be able to save between 30% and 40% of the cost of the insurance when you deduct it. This means that a policy that costs $600 a year will actually only cost you $360 to $420.

Here are the deductions that apply to a sole proprietor or a one-person LLC (there are different rules for partnerships and corporations—see chapter 17).

- Business liability insurance and homeowners liability endorsement: The cost of these policies is 100% deductible as a business expense on **Schedule C Profit or Loss from Business.**

- Car insurance: You can deduct the business-use percent of this cost on **Schedule C** if you use the actual cost method of claiming car expenses. If you use the standard mileage rate you can't deduct your car insurance, since that rate already includes the estimated cost of car insurance.

- Disability income insurance: If you deduct the cost of this insurance you will have to pay income tax on any benefits that you receive later, so we don't recommend that you deduct it.

- Health insurance: If you aren't eligible to be covered by medical insurance through an employer, you can deduct 100% of your premiums on **Form 1040 Individual Income Tax Return.** If you set up an HRA for your spouse-employee, you can deduct 100% of medical expenses paid under this plan on **Schedule C.**

- Homeowners insurance and renter's insurance: You can claim your Time-Space percentage of this cost as a deduction on **Form 8829 Business Use of Your Home.**

- Life insurance: This cost isn't deductible unless you incorporate. Consult a tax professional for this complex area.

- Long-term care insurance: Portions of your premiums may be deductible on **Form 1040,** depending on your age and the cost of the premiums.

- Umbrella liability insurance: You can deduct your Time-Space percentage of this cost as a deduction on **Form 8829.**

- Workers' compensation insurance: This cost is 100% deductible as a business expense on **Schedule C.**

For more information about how to take these business deductions, consult the *Tax Workbook and Organizer*.

Working with an Insurance Agent

It's important to develop a good working relationship with your insurance agent(s). Your agent's job is to match your insurance needs with the best available insurance policies, which plays an important role in protecting your livelihood. You want to have an insurance agent who is more experienced in selling business than personal insurance, and who sells to many other family child care providers. An agent who understands family child care can help you find the best policy and advise you as your insurance needs change.

Once you find a good agent, it's a good idea to purchase as many of your different business and personal insurance policies as you can from that person. That way, she can better understand all your risks and help you prepare for them.

To get the most from your insurance policies, you need to work closely with your insurance agent. This means being completely open with your agent about your business to ensure that she understands all the risks associated with your business that need to be covered.

Whenever there is any major change in your life (marriage, divorce, the birth of a child, a new home, a child leaves for college) you should discuss the changes with your insurance agent and ask her to reevaluate your insurance needs. This may seem reckless at a time when the homeowners and car insurance policies of many providers aren't being renewed simply because they operate a family child care business (although the provider may have faithfully paid her premiums for years without making a single claim). However, if you don't tell your agent about the risks you are facing, she can't protect you from them.

Some providers have told us, "My insurance agent tells me that he doesn't want to know that I'm doing family child care." This is a recipe for disaster, because it means that you probably won't be covered if there is a claim.

Insurance is complicated, so don't expect to understand what your insurance policies cover unless you ask questions. If you don't understand something, ask your agent. Your agent or your policy may use unfamiliar language (such as "aggregate limit" or "first dollar payer") and you may get easily confused. Don't hesitate to ask your agent to explain your policies to you in a way that you can fully understand. One sign of a good agent is someone who will take the time to help you.

Not communicating with your insurance agent can have serious consequences. What if you're already caring for the maximum number of children allowed under your license, and a desperate parent begs you to care for her child for a week because her regular caregiver is ill? This may be illegal under your state's licensing law or there may be an exception that allows you to be overenrolled for a few days. But regardless of the licensing rules, if there's an accident in your program during this time, you may not be covered by your business liability insurance policy. If you are regularly overenrolled, and an accident happens, you probably won't be covered, and your policy isn't likely to be renewed. If you're communicating with your insurance agent about the times when you are overenrolled, you can get important advice about whether you will be covered if there is a problem.

If a parent ever says to you, "I'm going to sue you," you should immediately talk to your agent and explain what happened. As a general rule, let your agent know what is going on and use her as a resource to help you defuse any problems or tell you how to best protect yourself.

Keep Your Policy from Being Dropped

In general, if an insurance company decides that they no longer want to cover the risks of your business they won't cancel you; instead, they simply won't renew your policy. When one of your insurance policies isn't renewed, this will cause you problems for years to come. Whenever you apply for new insurance coverage you will be asked if another company ever dropped your policy. If you answer yes, you will have a much harder time finding a new insurance company to insure you.

Your insurance agent should work hard to prevent your policies from being dropped like this. Although the state laws vary, your insurance company will probably be required to give you a certain number of weeks' notice that your policy won't be renewed. (If your company isn't an admitted carrier in your state, it may not have to follow those rules.)

Filing a Claim

Insurance is one of the few purchases that we hope we will never use. But if you do suffer a loss or injury, it pays to carefully assess the situation to make sure that it makes sense to submit a claim. If the cost of the repair will be less than or close to the amount of your deductible, it makes sense to pay it yourself rather than to file a claim.

If this is your second claim in a year, the company may be more likely to not renew your policy if you submit it. Be especially careful about filing claims that deal with property damage. If you have a fire in your home that destroys $40,000 worth of your personal and business property, you shouldn't hesitate to make a claim. However, if someone steals your TV and VCR, it may not be wise to file a claim. In general, you shouldn't file any property claims for less than $500. Look at your insurance as a way to protect you against financial disaster, not as a protection for every piece of property you own.

However, bear in mind that your business liability and homeowners insurance policies will probably require you to report any incident that could turn into a claim, usually within one year of the incident. You need to understand the rules about reporting incidents to your insurance company. Ask your agent about what you need to report and what information may or may not be held against you.

Unfortunately, some insurance companies will be looking for reasons not to insure people. Before you make a claim, find out if there will be any consequences for doing so. If you're considering making a claim on your homeowners or car insurance, it may not be a good idea to talk to your insurance agent about it. For these policies, just asking your agent about your insurance coverage may be a cause for the company to drop your policy. It's better to call a different agent from the same company to ask your question anonymously (don't give them your name or policy number). This won't be a problem with business liability insurance.

Don't hesitate to contact your business liability insurance agent about any questions that you have about making a claim on your policy.

Insurance companies keep track of your claims history, especially for homeowners and car insurance. In fact, all homeowners claims are kept in a central location that all the companies can access. This system tracks all the claims that are made by an address.

Before you purchase a home, you should ask your homeowners insurance agent to check this database to find out the history of the claims on that house. If there are a lot of past claims on the home, it may be difficult to get homeowners insurance.

You may also have a more difficult time getting insurance if you are buying a home just for your business and don't plan to live in it. It pays to check to see if you can get insurance before you buy.

Provide Full Information

Insurance companies may refuse to pay a claim if you failed to disclose or gave false information on an application. For example, let's say that you're applying for life insurance and claim that you don't use tobacco, but you actually do. You will probably be found out, since most insurance companies require you to submit blood and urine samples and will screen them for tobacco use. Insurance companies will also require you to let them access your medical records. So be sure to disclose all your health history to your agent, even if you know that it may cause the insurance company to decline you.

If your homeowners insurance agent doesn't know you are running a child care business in your home, you run the risk that any claims for damages may be denied. If you hear that your homeowners company isn't renewing other providers, or if you read that your policy specifically excludes family child care, start shopping for insurance coverage from another company.

Canceling a Policy

Usually you can cancel a policy at any time and get a refund for part of the unused amount. For example, if you paid your business liability policy for the entire year and went out of business six months later, you should notify your company, cancel your policy, and request a refund. Since some policies have cancellation fees or a nonrefundable minimum premium, you may not receive the entire remaining amount as a refund.

If you decide to change insurance companies, make sure that you are covered under the new policy before you contact your old policy for a refund. If you watch this closely, you can avoid paying for double coverage.

When You Close Your Business

You should reevaluate your insurance coverage after (or before, if possible) any major transition in your life, such as a marriage, a divorce, the birth of a child, a move, or a death in your family. Closing your child care business is another one of those transitions; you should talk to your insurance agent and discuss your changing insurance needs. Here are some steps that you should take when you close your child care business:

- Contact your licensor and ask how to remove your name from the list of licensed child care providers.
- Contact your state's secretary of state office and ask how to relinquish your business name, if you have one.
- Ask your insurance agent if you are entitled to any refunds on your discontinued business insurance policies.
- If you have a business liability endorsement on your homeowners policy (see page 65), cancel it and review your homeowners insurance coverage.
- Discuss your new circumstances with your insurance agent and decide what insurance protection you need.
- Consult the *Tax Workbook and Organizer* for information about how going out of business will affect your taxes.

PART III

Handling Legal Issues

CHAPTER TWELVE

Custody, Privacy, and Confidentiality

Chapter Summary
This chapter discusses the legal issues associated with custody and privacy and
confidentiality, and explains how to handle them.

As a family child care provider, you are so deeply involved in the lives of the children in
your care that it may seem as if you are a member of the family. Although this close interaction usually offers benefits to everyone involved, it can also raise sensitive issues in the
areas of custody and privacy and confidentiality.

Child Custody Issues
One of the situations that can put you in a difficult position is when the parents of a child in
your care become enmeshed in a custody dispute. This doesn't happen only when parents
are in the process of divorcing; it can also arise in cases where the parents never married or
if one of the parents is losing parental rights for any reason. As the child's provider, you are
likely to be drawn into any battles between the parents, and it is important that you understand the basic rules about handling these kinds of situations.

Custodial Rights
Let's say that the mother of one of the children in your care comes to you and says, "My
husband and I are in the process of getting a divorce. I'm afraid that he might take our child
and flee to another state, so I don't want you to allow him to pick her up anymore." What
should you do in this case? What is your legal responsibility? Although state laws vary, most
of them include the following types of parental rights:

- **Legal custody.** The parent who has legal custody has the power to make decisions about
  the child's health and welfare, usually including the right to enroll the child in a child
  care program.

- **Physical custody.** The parent who has physical custody lives with the child and is responsible for the child's food, clothing, shelter, and well-being on a daily basis. (You really want to know who has legal custody; that's more important than physical custody.)
- **Joint custody.** In this situation, the parents are sharing legal and/or physical custody of the child.

Usually the parent who has physical custody will also have legal custody of a child. Joint physical custody means that the child spends some time with each parent. If one parent has sole legal and physical custody, the court will usually grant visitation rights for the noncustodial parent, including allowing that parent to pick up the child from a child care program.

Both birth parents are sometimes entitled to both legal and physical custody of a child—including the right to pick up the child from a child care program at any time—unless a court order has limited those rights. Therefore, you should assume that both parents have full custody rights unless the other parent gives you a court order that says differently.

A parent will have custody rights even if that person isn't named as someone who is permitted to pick up the child on your authorized pickup list (see pages 45–48). In other words, one parent can't limit the rights of the other parent. However, if a parent gives you a copy of a court order (such as a divorce decree or a restraining order) that limits the rights of the other parent, you must follow that order. For example, if the court order says that the father only has physical custody of the child on Monday and Wednesday, then you must only allow him to pick up the child on those days.

So in the above case where the mother asked you not to let the father pick up the child, you would have to answer, "I'm sorry, but my understanding is that both parents have a right to pick up the child. I can't prevent the father from picking up the child without some kind of court order that limits his custody rights. If you can show me that, I will be happy to follow its directions." Make sure that the mother understands that it is her responsibility to get a court order and show it to you before you can follow her instructions. If you are unclear about what the court order says, ask the parent to clarify it. Make a copy of the court document, and keep it for your own records.

Legal Guardians and Grandparents

A legal guardian is a person who has been granted legal and physical custody of a child by a court—if a child has a legal guardian, the birth parents will no longer have custody. (In this case, if a birth parent tries to pick up the child, you should refuse and immediately try to contact the legal guardian.) Only a child's parents or legal guardians have custodial rights. Although a custodial parent or guardian may authorize a grandparent to pick up a child from your care, grandparents don't have a legal right to do so unless a court has granted that person custody or visitation rights.

Ask about Custody When You Enroll Each Child

You should not let anyone pick up a child from your program unless that person either has physical custody of the child or is authorized by a person who has physical custody to pick up the child. To reduce any misunderstandings later, when a child is enrolled in your program, you need to ask the following:

- What is the legal relationship of each parent to the child?
- Does anyone else (another parent, stepparent, adoptive parent, guardian, or court-ordered custodian) have a legal relationship to the child?
- If the parents aren't living together, get copies of the court documents that state who has physical and legal custody and whether there are any court-ordered restraining orders.
- If there are such documents, tell the parents that you will need to have copies of any changes that are made in the custody arrangements for the child.
- If someone other than a parent enrolls a child in your program, ask for written authorization from one of the birth parents or a court order showing that the person has custody or guardianship rights.

Here's an example: A mother enrolls her child in your program, and when you ask about the child's father, she replies that they haven't lived together for years. However, she doesn't have a court order granting her sole physical custody of the child. Then one day a man shows up to get the child, and the child runs toward him, crying "Daddy!" What should you do? The answer will depend partly on whether the parents were ever married:

- If the parents were married, but haven't lived together for years, the father still has the same custody rights as the mother.
- If the parents were never married, the state laws vary. However, the father may have equal custody rights if he declared his paternity when the child was born.

In this scenario, you can't be sure that this man is the child's father, and you should do everything reasonable that you can to prevent the child from leaving with him. For example, you might stall him by asking him to wait while you contact the mother. If he insists on taking the child anyway, note his license plate and call the police immediately. Although you're obligated to protect the child's safety, your responsibility doesn't extend to trying to physically stop him from taking the child. If you act reasonably and he insists on taking the child without your permission, it's highly unlikely that you'll be held responsible.

When Parents Disagree or Become Disruptive

Although custodial parents and legal guardians can always pick up a child from your care, you have the right to refuse to allow anyone else to do so, including grandparents. Your business is like any other business, in the sense that you don't have to serve everyone. For example, if you were to become disruptive in a grocery store, you would be asked to leave. In the same way, if someone causes problems in your business, you can ask that person to leave (as long as you avoid illegal discrimination, as described in chapter 13).

For example, let's say that a boy's parents are divorced and share joint custody of him. Each parent gives you a list of the people who are authorized to pick up the boy, and the father authorizes his girlfriend to do so when it's his turn. This makes the mother very angry, and she asks you to refuse to let the girlfriend pick him up. In this case, you can do any of the following:

- Tell the father that you won't allow the girlfriend to pick up the child.
- Allow each parent to choose the authorized pickup people on their days.
- Ask the parents for a list of authorized people that they both agree upon.

It's up to you to make the decision, not the parent. Bear in mind that refusing to allow someone to pick up a child may not always be a good idea because of the potential for creating conflicts with parents. However, if the parents continue to try to put you in the middle of their arguments, you can refuse to continue taking care of their child.

Handling Legal Disputes between Parents

If the parents of a child become embroiled in a serious legal dispute, you may want to avoid taking sides. One parent may want you to testify on his or her behalf or to provide negative information about the other parent for use in court. However, you don't have to answer any questions from a lawyer unless you want to or you are subpoenaed to testify.

In some custody disputes, the court will order the parents to transfer their custody of the child at a neutral location—and the location that they select may be the child care provider's home. If you believe that this would be too disruptive for your business, or if you just don't want to be around when both parents are present, you can usually refuse to allow your home to be used for this purpose.

If the police or a child protection worker show up at your home and ask to take a child, this will most likely be due to a child abuse investigation. Whenever any government official asks to speak to a child or to take a child, you should always do the following:

- Insist on examining the person's identification (with a photograph).
- Call the person's office number to verify his or her identify.
- Write down the person's name and badge number.
- Call the parent as soon as you can to inform them of what has happened.
- Call your licensor.

Privacy and Confidentiality

Privacy is becoming an increasingly valuable commodity, and we are all trying to protect our own privacy as much as possible. In addition, family child care providers have a professional responsibility to vigilantly protect the privacy of the families of the children in their care. It can be difficult to keep from revealing any information about your clients in a business that's as personal as family child care. But it's important. Here are some examples of the kinds of situations that could raise privacy concerns in your business:

- You post photographs of the children in your care on your refrigerator, on a bulletin board in your entryway, or in a photo album that you show to prospective parents during parent interviews.

- A school counselor calls you and asks about the recent behavior of one of the children in your care.
- A parent gives you the name of her previous provider as a reference; you call this previous caregiver and ask if the parent was a good client.
- One of your employees overhears some information about a child in your care. Later, the parent of another child asks her, "I've heard that one of the children may need an operation soon. Is it true?"
- You hear a child in your care telling her mother that another child told her that her parents are going to get a divorce.
- You use an electronic monitor to listen in on a sleeping baby.
- Your own child tells the children in your care that your family just inherited some money.

Know Your State's Privacy Laws

Some states have specific privacy and confidentiality regulations that apply to family child care providers, such as these:

- Tennessee (Rule 1240-4-4.02): The licensee and caregivers shall not disclose or knowingly permit the use of by other persons any information concerning a child or family except as required by law or regulation.

- Massachusetts (102CMR8.15): Information contained in a child's record shall be privileged and confidential. The provider shall not distribute or release information in a child's record to any unauthorized person without the written consent of the child's parent.

State laws often require providers to share any requested information with specific governmental agencies, such as the police or the child care licensing agency. Ask your licensor to learn about the state laws that affect you. Make sure that you know the law, so that you don't make any mistakes in sharing private information.

However, even if your state doesn't have a specific law that deals with privacy and confidentiality, you need to be very sensitive to parent concerns in this area. The parents of the children in your care put their trust in you and have a high expectation that you will keep information about their children and their family private and confidential. It's a sign of professionalism to reward this trust and protect their privacy. A parent whose privacy is violated will be more likely to spread negative information about your program or even initiate a lawsuit against you.

Even if you aren't bound by a state privacy law, you should assume that all information about the children in your care and their families is confidential and should not be disclosed. This includes the names of the children in your care and their parents. Since this information remains confidential even after a client leaves your program, you can't disclose the names of any of your former clients, either.

• •

An Unusual Case

Minnesota licensing law states that a "provider shall not disclose any records on children in care to any persons other than the parents of the child" (except for specified government agencies and medical officials). One Minnesota provider got into trouble when this law was applied to an unusual situation. She had formerly cared for a child whose mother had custody and whose father had a history of stalking the mother. The father's new girlfriend called the provider and used false pretenses to find out the name of the child's new caregiver. The father then used this information to begin stalking the mother again.

The state licensing agency took negative action against the provider for revealing this information. She appealed, saying that the law didn't apply to this situation because she was no longer the child's provider. However, the agency interpreted the law to mean that a provider wasn't allowed to share any information about a child, even about a new caregiver.

• •

It's always safest to assume that your clients don't want you to share any information about them with anyone—friend, neighbor, or relative. In addition to obviously personal information, this also means that you shouldn't reveal anything else, including the following:

- The name of the client's boyfriend
- What kind of car she drives
- That she is receiving food stamps
- That you saw her at Wal-Mart last weekend
- That her mother is diabetic
- What kind of shoes she wears

As a rule, parents don't want you to share any information at all about them with anyone, unless they give you specific permission to do so. Bear in mind that when you share information, the person you tell is likely to share it again. The information—and the fact that it was you who revealed it—may eventually reach your client's best friend or worst enemy. This means that you shouldn't even talk about your clients with the members of your immediate family.

Protecting your clients' privacy also means being discreet when you run into a client in a public location, such as a shopping mall, post office, movie theater, or restaurant. In this situation, you shouldn't approach the client, but rather wait for her to approach you. She may not want to advertise to other people that she uses child care services. Although this may seem extreme, it can be an issue for some people, and it's best to play it safe.

One provider saw the father of one of the children in her care while shopping at the mall, and noticed that he was with a woman who wasn't his wife. Although it was difficult, she kept quiet about what she had seen. The parents later divorced.

What if you get a call from a counselor at a child's school who wants to know how the child is behaving in your program, or a family court mediator who wants to interview you about one of the parents? The best approach is to explain that you can't say anything about the child or the parent unless you have written permission from the parent to do so. You can either ask this person to get the permission from the parent or you can contact the parent yourself to get it.

What if you tell a parent that her child was bitten by another child in your program, and she wants to know who did it? Explain to the parent that it's your policy is to keep this information confidential, because protecting the children's privacy is in the best interest of everyone involved. (Biting is not a problem that should be addressed by public shame or punishment; you should report any biting incidents to your licensing worker.)

• •

Child Care Consultations

You can always call another provider or an outside expert to discuss a behavior problem that you're having with a child in your program (such as biting other children). However, be careful to refer to the child simply as "a boy," rather than "Joey," since someone may know who "Joey" is. You can share more identifiable information if the parents give you permission to do so, but don't just assume that they will allow this; always get their permission first.

• •

Adopt a Written Privacy Policy

To help alleviate parental concerns about confidential information, it's a good idea to include a written privacy policy with your other policies (see appendix A). This can be a simple statement, such as:

> I will do all that I can to protect your family's privacy and I will abide by our state's privacy law. In addition, I will keep all records and information about your child and your family private and confidential, unless I have your written permission to reveal specific information. I ask that you also respect the privacy of my family by not sharing any information you learn about my family with others, without my written permission.

Employees, helpers, or volunteers who work with the children in your care may also be exposed to confidential information in your home. They may have access to the children's medical records, or they may become aware of a child's medical condition through direct observation. Explain the need for privacy and your commitment to privacy and confidentiality to everyone who may come into contact with the children in your care. Discuss your privacy policy with your employees and volunteers, and make sure that they understand it. Tell them that following it is a requirement for working in your business.

Use Permission Forms

You should be alert for the many ways in which information about the children in your care may be exposed to other people, for example:

- Placing photos of the children in your home
- Posting the full names of children on a bulletin board
- Allowing parents to pass out birthday party invitations to the other children
- Inviting neighboring children over to play during child care hours

Most of the time you will be able to handle any parental privacy concerns about something you would like to do by simply asking the parents to sign a written permission form. For example, if you would like to use an electronic monitor to listen in on a sleeping baby, ask the parent if this is okay. (Also, check with your licensor to see if monitors are permitted.)

The best way to get permissions is to ask the parents to sign a simple permission form. Ask your licensor for advice about the language that you should use on this form. You can include a general permission form as part of your policies. For an example of such a permission form, see appendix A.

You can also have the parents sign a customized permission form for a specific purpose:

I, _____ (full name of parent), hereby give permission for _____ (full name of provider) to discuss with _____ (name of school counselor, court mediator, psychologist, and so on) the firsthand information that she has about _____ (full name of child).

_____ (parent signature) _____ (date)

Having a privacy policy and using the appropriate permission forms are not just good ways to handle privacy and confidentiality issues. They also help you maintain good communication with parents, which will help you avoid any problems later on (see chapter 3).

Helping Others Keep Confidences

At times, someone else in your home may overhear sensitive information about the families of the children in your care—for example, about a medical condition, a marital separation, or a financial situation. Those who are hearing the information may be your employees or unpaid helpers, the parents of the children in your care, the children in your care, or even your own children. Those who are passing on the information may be the parents or children involved. (If they are sharing information about themselves, they can't say that their privacy has been violated. However, if someone else overhears and repeats what they have said, then you may be held responsible.)

Whatever the circumstances, you should be concerned about the spread of any confidential information in your home, and there are some steps that you can take to reduce the likelihood that the privacy of the families in your care will be violated:

- Explain your privacy policy and your commitment to confidentiality to all employees, helpers, or volunteers who work with the children in your care, and ask them to follow it.

- Share your expectations about privacy with the parents of the children in your care and ask them for their expectations. Share any specific concerns that you have and listen closely to the parent's wishes. Explain that you may be required to share certain information about their families with your licensing worker or other government agencies.

- Consider adding the following language in discussing your privacy policy with your clients:

  My home is a safe place for children and their families. Occasionally children or parents may share personal information with each other. My policy is to respect the privacy of your family, and I also expect you to respect the privacy of my family and the other families in my program. This means not sharing any sensitive or personal information that may be revealed during conversations in my home. I would also appreciate it if you would talk to your children, when appropriate, about keeping confidences and respecting the privacy of all the families in the program.

- When appropriate, talk to the children in your care about privacy. If you overhear a child proclaim to her mother at pickup time that "Suzie had diarrhea!" you may want to have a private conversation with the mother about how to deal with this.

- When appropriate, talk with your own children about keeping confidences. Ask them to come to you before they share anything that they overhear with other people, or if they have any questions about confidential information.

Protecting Your Own Privacy

Like everyone else, family child care providers want to protect their own privacy and that of their family. As you discuss the issues of privacy and confidentiality with parents, express any concerns that you have about your own privacy, and ask the parents to respect your wishes to protect it. The best way to do this is to use your policies and behavior to set a good example of how to protect confidential information.

To protect yourself against identity theft, we suggest that you get a taxpayer identification number and use it instead of your Social Security number when parents claim the child care and dependent care credits. To get this number, fill out **Form SS-4 Application for Employer Identification Number.** You can get this form on our Web site or you can fill it out online at the IRS Web site (www.irs.gov). You can also call the IRS at 866-816-2065. For more information, see the *Tax Workbook and Organizer*.

• •

Parent Social Security Numbers

Some providers ask parents for their Social Security numbers so that they can find anyone who leaves without paying. We don't believe that this is a good practice. Just as you should protect your own privacy by not releasing your own Social Security number to parents, you shouldn't expect parents to release their number to you. You can protect yourself from parents who leave without paying by requiring payment at least a week in advance and requiring an advance deposit for the last two weeks of care (see pages 16–17).

• •

Slander

Slander is when you tell someone something that damages a third person's reputation. (*Libel* is when you put this kind of information in writing.) Although slander is illegal, it's rarely the subject of lawsuits. In addition, you can't be sued for slander if the information that you shared was true. However, even though you are unlikely to be sued, you want to avoid passing on defamatory information, because you don't want to get a reputation as a gossip; as a professional, you should be discreet.

The most common area where a family child care provider is likely to encounter the issue of slander is in handling references and referrals (see page 125).

If You Are Slandered by a Parent

Some providers have had the unpleasant experience of dealing with a parent who, after leaving their program, has spread false gossip about her to other families in the community, claiming that the provider neglected or abused the parent's child. This kind of gossip can be damaging to your business.

If this happens to you, the first thing you should do is immediately contact your licensor and share your side of the story before the parent makes a formal complaint against you. Next, you may want to tell all the parents in your care that an unhappy former client is spreading false information about you. Don't go into specifics about what you've heard. Just ask the parents to contact you immediately if the gossipy parent tries to talk to them, or they hear any rumors from someone else.

In our experience, parents who spread gossip and rumors only do so for a short period, usually no more than several weeks. After that, nothing more happens. Although it can be a painful experience to be the subject of slander, the best approach is usually to just wait for it to die down. It's extremely difficult to successfully sue someone for slander, and you shouldn't attempt this without consulting a lawyer. If you're concerned that someone is continuing to spread rumors about you that are harmful to your business, you may want to write a letter to that person. The letter should be businesslike, simply stating what you've heard and politely asking the person to stop spreading the rumor.

References and Referrals

There are several ways that the issue of getting or giving references may come up in your business, and all of them bring up issues of privacy and confidentiality. The simplest situation is when you wish to give a parent's name to prospective clients as a reference. In this case, simply ask for written permission to use the client as a reference. However, you may also ask for references from prospective clients, or you may be called by another provider because a parent has given your name as a reference—and these situations bring up more complex confidentiality issues.

Getting References for Prospective Clients

It's reasonable to ask a prospective client to provide a reference from a previous child care provider. If the parent doesn't want to give you the name of the child's previous caregiver, you should seriously consider not accepting the child into your program.

If the parent gives you the name, and you call the previous caregiver, you can ask anything that you want. However, it's best to simply ask these questions:

- How long did you provide care for this child?
- What can you tell me about this child or the parent(s) that will help me meet their needs?
- If you had the choice, would you provide care again for this family?

You aren't responsible for anything that the previous caregiver says unless you repeat it to someone else. For example, if the parent's reference tells you something slanderous or damaging to the parent's reputation (such as "The father takes drugs," or "The mother neglects the child"), you aren't guilty of slander unless you repeat it. (See page 124 for a definition of slander.)

Giving References for Former Clients

What if you're called by another provider who's been given your name as a reference by a former client? You need to be extremely careful in this situation. First, you should answer no questions, or even acknowledge that you once provided care for this person, until you have a written permission signed by the parent. So the first thing you should say is, "It's my policy not to share any information about the families I have cared for. I can't even confirm that I provided care for this family. Please give me your phone number and send me a copy of a permission form signed by the parent, and I will call you back."

But even if you have permission to talk with the new provider, you may not want to. There's no law that requires you to answer any questions at all, and you may decide that it's not worth the risk of getting into trouble for what you might say. In this case, it's acceptable to respond to inquiries by simply saying, "I can't confirm that I provided care for this family, and I have a policy of not sharing any information about my previous clients, even with their permission."

If you do choose to talk about a previous client, there are some guidelines that you should follow in order to avoid trouble:

- Stick to facts that you know are true. Don't say, "I've heard that the parents drink a lot," or "The mother said that the father was in jail for six months for drugs." These are rumors that may or may not be true.

- Be specific, not general, in your comments. Say, "The mother paid me late three times last year," rather than "The mother was a deadbeat." Don't characterize: "The father was irresponsible." Stick to specific facts that you know are true. Say, "The mother picked up the child 95% of the time," or "The father called me, on average, three times a day to a see if the child was okay."

- The most telling comment that you can make to the new provider is whether you would provide care for this family again. Just say either, "I would provide care again for this family," or "I would not provide care again for this family." That's all that the new provider really needs to know.

Making Referrals to Other Providers

If you don't have any room in your program, a parent who's looking for child care may ask you to refer her to another provider. This brings up some issues that are similar to those involved in giving references. However, you don't need to worry if you follow some commonsense guidelines:

- Always ask permission before giving out the name of another provider.
- Don't say anything about another provider that might violate her privacy. Don't share any unnecessary information, such as details about her family.
- Don't say anything that makes it sound as if you're recommending a particular provider. Otherwise the parent may make a complaint against you later for referring someone who turns out to be a disaster.
- Give the parent the names of at least two providers, if possible, to avoid appearing to recommend a particular one.

When you give out names of other providers, you are making a referral, not a recommendation. Don't characterize a provider by describing her in terms that you can't prove, for example, by saying: "She'll be perfect for your child," "No one has ever filed a complaint against her," or "She takes wonderful field trips to the park every week."

The more you praise another provider, the more the parent will think that you're promising that her child will be happy there—and if the relationship doesn't work out, the parent may blame you. Instead, just pass on the contact information for some other providers in your area: "Here are the names of some providers who may have an opening. You may want to talk with them to see if any of them would be right for your child."

Nonpayment Hotlines

Some family child care associations keep a list of nonpaying parents that providers can call to find out if there's a problem with a prospective parent's payment history. We don't think this is a good idea. First, these lists are usually unreliable because they aren't up to date. Second, they're often inaccurate. For example:

- A parent may have paid her bill right after her name was turned in to the hotline.
- A parent may have paid on time, but had a conflict with her provider, who submitted false information to the hotline.
- There may be confusion over names that are common in the area.

If an association gives out a parent's name in these situations, it may be guilty of slander. Also, maintaining a nonpayment hotline isn't professional. It gives the impression that providers are blacklisting parents and creates a climate of distrust. Instead, we believe that you should collect payment from parents in advance, as described on pages 16–17. For more information, see *Family Child Care Contracts and Policies*.

CHAPTER THIRTEEN

Disabilities, Discrimination, and Price Fixing

Chapter Summary
This chapter covers what you need to know in order to comply with the federal regulations associated with disabilities, discrimination, and price fixing.

M any family child care providers aren't familiar with the regulatory requirements of the Americans with Disabilities Act or the laws that prohibit discrimination and price fixing. However, failing to comply with these federal regulations poses a legal risk to your business and makes you more vulnerable to potential lawsuits.

The Americans with Disabilities Act
The Americans with Disabilities Act of 1990 (ADA) is a major civil rights law that was passed to protect individuals with disabilities from discrimination. (Much of this information is adapted from the publications of the Child Care Law Center; see appendix B for more information.)

Who Is Covered by the ADA?
According to the ADA, a person is considered to have a disability if he or she has a physical or mental impairment that significantly limits one or more major life activities, such as hearing, seeing, learning, speaking, or walking. Examples of the covered impairments include, but aren't limited to, the following:

- Cancer
- Cerebral palsy
- Deafness
- Diabetes
- Emotional or mental illness
- Epilepsy

- HIV and AIDS
- Learning disabilities
- Mental retardation
- Multiple sclerosis
- Muscular dystrophy

In addition to these impairments, a person would also be covered by ADA under the following circumstances:

- The person has a history of a disability. (For example, leukemia that is currently in remission.)
- The person may be perceived by others as having a disability. (For example, diabetes that is controlled through medication.)
- The person is associated with a person who has a disability. (For example, you may not discriminate against a child because her mother has HIV or a mental illness.)

Short-term illnesses such as chicken pox, measles, the flu, or a cold are not considered to be disabilities or covered by the ADA.

• •

Check Your State Laws
In addition to the federal ADA, your state may also have its own laws that cover the rights of individuals with disabilities. These state laws may stipulate greater protections for these individuals and create greater responsibilities for child care providers. Ask your licensor or child care resource and referral agency about any state laws.

• •

Complying with the ADA
Only child care centers that are run by a religious organization are clearly exempt from the ADA. Other than that, all licensed, certified, and registered child care programs are required to comply with the ADA. You must comply even if you aren't receiving any government subsidies, such as state child care assistance programs or the USDA Food Program. (It isn't clear if family child care providers who are exempt from state regulations or are operating illegally must also comply.)

Complying with the ADA means that you cannot discriminate against children who have special needs. Although it doesn't require you to care for all children who have disabilities, you can't refuse to care for a child with a disability for the following reasons:

- The child has a severe disability.
- You don't feel that you have the skill or ability to care for this child.
- Your written contract or policies state that you don't care for children with disabilities.
- You just don't feel comfortable dealing with certain disabilities, such as AIDS.

In general, you must do whatever is reasonable to accommodate children with special needs in your program. You must evaluate each child's individual needs and try to find a reasonable way to accommodate them. If a visually impaired child needs large-print books, audio-recorded books, or books in Braille, you will probably be required to provide them. These adaptations are usually simple and involve little or no cost to you.

There are only four circumstances in which you can refuse to provide care to a child who has a disability:

- If the child needs special equipment or services, providing them would impose an *undue burden* on your program, and there are no reasonable alternatives. The ADA defines an "undue burden" as a significant difficulty or expense. Let's say that you are asked to care for a child who is Deaf and needs a full-time interpreter. You should explore alternatives, such as learning sign language yourself, finding volunteer interpreters at a local college, or some other solution. However, if none of these alternatives meet the child's needs, and a full-time interpreter would cost you $300 a week, this may be an undue burden to you.

- If the child's condition poses a *direct threat* (as defined by the ADA) to the other children or yourself, and there is no reasonable way to eliminate the threat by changing your policies or practices. For example, let's say that a child with AIDS has open, oozing, infectious lesions. You consult the child's doctor (with the parent's permission), and she advises you that the lesions pose a direct threat to the other children in your care that cannot be eliminated by changes in your program.

- If the child's condition requires you to make an architectural change that isn't *readily achievable*, and there are no reasonable alternatives. "Readily achievable" is defined as able to be carried out without much difficulty or expense. If the only way to make your program accessible to a child in a wheelchair was to build a $7,000 entrance ramp or spend $4,000 widening your doorways and remodeling your bathroom, most likely you would not be required to make these modifications. However, if you can accommodate the child by carrying him up the front steps and using a smaller indoor wheelchair, then you must do so.

• •

Tax Incentives for ADA Compliance

There's a federal tax credit and deduction that you can take advantage of when you incur expenses to comply with ADA requirements. You can use these tax benefits for the costs involved in removing architectural and transportation barriers, building ramps, hiring interpreters or readers, buying taped texts, and modifying your equipment, among other things. For more information, see the *Family Child Care Tax Workbook and Organizer* or IRS **Publication 907.**

• •

- If accommodating the child would require changes that would *fundamentally alter* the nature of your program, and there are no reasonable alternatives. Let's say that you are asked to care for a child who has a severe case of attention deficit disorder. The child requires full-time, one-to-one supervision, and to accommodate that you would have to hire an assistant at $300 a week. You should look for volunteers who can help you, but if you are unsuccessful, you would not be required to provide care for this child. However, if the child's condition were less severe and you were able to manage the child along with the other children in your care, then you would have to accept him.

You aren't allowed to charge a family more for providing care to a child who has special needs. However, you can raise your rates for all the children in your care to cover the additional costs associated with that child. You can't raise your rates for that child alone, even if you have to spend more time and effort caring for her than the other children.

The only exception to this is that you can charge more if the child is receiving professional services (such as physical therapy or speech therapy) from an outside service provider while attending your program. In this case you can charge the parents directly for the cost of the special services.

If the child's parents volunteer to pay you more to care for the child, you may accept their payment. However, you should get a note from them stating they are volunteering to pay you extra. You can never ask parents to pay more, and you should make it clear that they aren't legally obligated to do so.

Disclosing Information about Disabilities

Parents aren't required to tell you that their child has a disability. In an interview, you can't directly ask a parent, "Does your child have a disability?" However, you can ask, "Does your child have any medical conditions or special needs that I should be aware of to better accommodate her needs?"

After a child is admitted to your program, you may request his or her health records, but if you do, you must request the same records for all the children in your care. In addition, you must use the information you receive to help you meet the child's needs, not to exclude the child because she has a disability.

You must keep all medical information that you receive for any child confidential unless the parent gives you explicit (and preferably written) permission to share it with someone else.

If a parent doesn't disclose a child's disability to you, and you have no fair reason to believe that a child has a disability, then you would not be in violation of the ADA if you were to refuse to enroll the child or to terminate her care.

If you have reason to believe that a child has a disability, but the parents won't discuss the child's condition, then you must continue to provide care only if you can do so in a way that is appropriate and safe for all the children in your care. If the child's condition—for example, extremely aggressive behavior or limited responsiveness—is such that you believe professional help is needed, and the parent continues to be uncooperative, you aren't required to continue to care for the child.

Getting Help and Answers

Caring for a child with disabilities is mostly a matter of taking reasonable steps to accommodate the child's individual needs. Before you terminate or refuse to enroll such a child, try taking the following steps:

- Seek the advice of an objective professional (nurse, doctor, school counselor, lawyer, and so on).
- Contact the Department of Justice's toll-free ADA Information Line (800-514-0301 voice; 800-514-0383 TTY), which answers questions and provides information about ADA requirements.
- Contact the organizations that support individuals who have particular disabilities, such as the United Cerebral Palsy Association, the Cystic Fibrosis Foundation, the Epilepsy Foundation of America, and so on.
- Ask your local United Way for a referral. This organization may be able to answer your questions or help you identify additional resources.

Children with HIV and AIDS

Some family child care providers are concerned that children who are HIV-positive or have AIDS are protected under the ADA. You can allay these fears by consulting the resources listed in appendix B to find out more about how HIV is spread and how to protect yourself and the other children in your care. For example, here's some information from "Caring for Children with HIV or AIDS in Child Care":

> HIV can only be transmitted through the exchange of certain body fluids. Many body fluids do not pose a problem unless they contain visible blood. Saliva, sweat, tears, vomit, urine, feces, nasal secretions, and breast milk all pose virtually no risk of transmission of the virus with casual contact, unless they contain visible blood. In the child care setting, contact with blood will be the main type of body fluid which will require using universal precautions.
>
> There are no known cases of children (or adults) having become infected with HIV through casual household contact, like food preparation, eating, hugging, kissing, diapering, or other forms of contact commonly occurring in the same household, or in child care. Even biting has never resulted in transmission of the virus in the child care setting. A child with HIV or AIDS poses virtually no risk to the health of the other children or staff in a child care setting. This is particularly true when universal infection control measures are taken on a regular basis for all children. Taking these simple precautions on a routine and uniform basis (such as regular hand washing) when caring for all children can protect both children and staff from transmission of HIV and other infections.

You can't require that a child be tested for HIV or that a parent tell you if a child has tested positive. Therefore, you should always assume that you could be caring for a child who is HIV-positive and follow the universal infection control measures to protect everyone in your program. These measures include avoiding direct contact with blood (using latex gloves), washing your hands regularly during the day, using a bleach solution to disinfect toys and surfaces, and disposing of waste that could carry infectious material.

For more information about universal infection control measures, contact your licensor, your local Occupational and Safety Health Administration office, or the Centers for Disease Control (see appendix B).

If a parent does reveal to you that her child is HIV-positive, you must keep this information strictly confidential unless you have written permission from the parent to disclose it. If another parent finds out that one of the children in your care is HIV-positive and demands that you remove that child, or they will remove their own child, you cannot terminate the infected child. The best approach is to take on the responsibility of helping to educate parents about HIV and AIDS, regardless of whether you are caring for any infected children.

If you have questions or need more information about how to provide safe, appropriate care for HIV-positive children, contact your licensor or your local child care resource and referral service.

Problems with Parents

Some family child care providers are afraid that the parents of a child with disabilities will sue the provider for being unable to meet the parent's idea of adequate services. Parents who have children with disabilities are looking for someone to provide quality care for their child, like any other parent. They aren't looking for excuses to sue you for refusing to provide adequate care. However, if a parent feels that you are discriminating against their child in violation of the ADA, they have several options:

- The parent can ask a local mediation service to provide a mediator to try to work out a voluntary solution to the problem.

- The parent can file a written complaint with the U.S. Department of Justice or the state department of human rights. These departments will investigate and attempt to resolve the problem through discussions with you and informal settlements. Although the government can file a lawsuit to seek money damages, to date this has never happened with a family child care provider.

- The parent can file a lawsuit to stop the discrimination. The court could order you to provide reasonable accommodations for the child, and the parents could win money damages against you for attorney's fees, emotional distress, and other expenses. Again, so far this has never happened.

As long as you are trying your best to accommodate the child's needs, and ask for help when you need it, it's unlikely that the parents will file a complaint against you.

Other ADA Issues

Business Liability Insurance

You can't refuse to care for a child with a disability because you fear that your business liability insurance rates will go up or your policy won't be renewed. You aren't obligated to inform your business liability insurance carrier that you are caring for a child with disabilities. However, if your insurance company specifically asks you about caring for children with special needs, you are obligated to answer their questions.

Your insurance company can exclude coverage for HIV and AIDS, raise your insurance premiums, or refuse to renew your policy because you're caring for a child with disabilities. It can refuse to cover you if it believes that the care required is beyond your capabilities or training or your home isn't properly outfitted for a child with a disability.

If you feel that you are being treated unfairly by your insurance company, you should make a written complaint to your agent. You can also make a complaint about unfair business practices to the office of your state insurance commissioner, your state attorney general, or your state department of human rights.

Landlords

If you rent, you and your landlord are both responsible for complying with the ADA, but the law doesn't specify exactly who is responsible for what. It seems reasonable that the landlord should be responsible for access to the building and the common areas, and that you should be responsible for making your rental unit accessible.

Before signing or renewing a lease or contract with your landlord, check to see if it spells out who is responsible for ADA compliance. If it says that you are responsible, that may be a danger sign. If there's no language in your lease about ADA compliance, negotiate with the landlord before you sign to clarify who will be responsible. You can ask for whatever terms you want, but at minimum the landlord should be responsible for bringing the access to the building and the common areas into compliance. If you plan to make permanent improvements to your living area, the lease may require you to seek the landlord's permission in writing.

New Homes and Room Additions

The ADA accessibility standards for an existing home only require you to remove any architectural barriers to the extent that is "readily achievable." In other words, if you have an existing playroom that isn't accessible, and it would cost you thousands of dollars to widen the doorways and build a ramp down the stairs to get into the room, then you wouldn't be required to do this, because it would be considered a significant expense.

However, the ADA has a different standard for new construction—room additions and new homes. If you make an addition to your home or build a new home and the new areas will be used for child care, then you must make them accessible to children with disabilities, regardless of the expense. In other words, if you build on a new playroom for your business, you are required to spend whatever it takes to make that room accessible.

If you buy a new home that isn't accessible, you aren't required to make it so. In this case, you will only be required to make any modifications that are "readily achievable." But if you build a new home, all the rooms that are used for your business must be accessible.

Before building a new home or an addition, inform your architect that the new construction must comply with ADA architectural standards. (See page 131 for a description of the federal tax credit that can help reduce the cost to you.) These are the most common changes that need to be made:

- Make entrances accessible by adding ramps and widening doors.
- Make program areas accessible by removing high-pile carpeting, using accessible door hardware, and widening doors.
- Make bathrooms accessible by widening doors and installing grab bars and raised toilet seats.

Hiring and the ADA

The federal ADA law prohibits employers who have 15 or more employees from discriminating against prospective employees who have disabilities. (Your state law may prohibit discrimination for businesses with fewer than 15 employees.) Even if your business is too small to fall under the discrimination laws, we recommend that you not discriminate in hiring. Under the ADA, you must make reasonable accommodations for an employee with a disability, unless doing so would impose an "undue hardship" on your program.

When interviewing prospective employees, you aren't allowed to ask if the person has a disability. However, you can ask if the person can perform the essential duties of the job, with or without reasonable accommodation. In your business, the essential duties might include being able to lift a two-year-old onto a diaper changing table several times a day or being able to carry the children outdoors in an emergency.

As a family child care provider, you know that every child has special needs of some kind. Every year tens of thousands of providers care for tens of thousands of children with disabilities without problems. Usually a provider can accommodate the child's needs by making a few simple adjustments in her program.

The more experience you have caring for children with special needs, the more you can promote your program as a high-quality place for all children. And by caring for children with disabilities you are setting a positive example for all the children in your care, their families, and your family, as well as complying with the law.

Discrimination

It's not always illegal to discriminate in your business. Sometimes it's okay to set different rules for different people, and sometimes it's not. Family child care providers often ask us when it's okay to treat their clients differently. For example:

- Can I tell a parent that I will no longer care for her child just because I don't like her rude attitude toward me? (Yes)

- Can I give one parent a discount on my rates, but not the others? (Sometimes)
- Can I put in my policies that I don't provide care for non-Christian families because of the religious education that I provide in my program? (No)
- Can I terminate a parent's contract because she made a complaint against me to my licensing worker? (Yes)
- Can I terminate a parent's contract without giving a reason? (Yes)

As you can see from these examples, in most situations you can set your own rules and run your business the way you want, without fear that you are breaking the law. You can refuse to enroll a child because the parent has bad personal hygiene. You can terminate a parent because her child is bullying the other children. You are the boss of your business, not the employee of the parent. (This is just an explanation of what you can do; we aren't recommending that you discriminate against individual parents just because you can.)

However, there are some kinds of discrimination that you can't engage in. Under federal law it is illegal to discriminate against either children or parents on the basis of their race, color, gender, religion, age, disability, or national origin.

In addition, your state or local government may outlaw discrimination based on marital status, sexual orientation, or some other attribute. If you provide care for low-income families who are subsidized by the state, your state contract may also make it illegal to discriminate against families who are receiving government assistance. This means that you may not refuse to provide care for a parent just because she is receiving subsidized assistance from your state. (For more information about your state's discrimination laws, contact the agency that regulates child care in your state, your state attorney general's office, your state department of human rights, or a lawyer.)

We are not recommending that you discriminate against anyone. However, there can be a lot of confusion about this issue, and it is important to understand the difference between legal and illegal discrimination, and how they might affect your business.

What Are the Discrimination Rules?

As we have seen, federal law prohibits discrimination on the basis of race, color, gender, religion, age, disability, or national origin. This means that you can't discriminate against a person because of her membership in one of these "protected classes." However, just because a family (or a person) is in a protected class doesn't mean that you can't discriminate against them for other reasons. You can discriminate as long as your reason for doing so is not based on their membership in a protected class. In other words:

- You cannot terminate a parent because she is Catholic. However, you can terminate her because she has violated your contract by not paying on time.
- You can offer religious training to the children in your care as part of your program, but you can't exclude a family from your program because they practice a different religion than you do.

- You can't refuse to accept a girl into your program because you want to enroll a boy to balance out your program.
- You can't discriminate against a child or parent because they have a disability, such as being HIV-positive, using a wheelchair, or having a chronic condition such as epilepsy. (See pages 129–34.)
- You can refuse to offer care to a parent because he works for a large corporation, but you can't exclude him because he comes from Mexico.

The prohibition against age discrimination usually only applies to people over age 40. (But state laws vary; in Minnesota it's illegal to discriminate against anyone over age 18 on the basis of age.) This means that in most states you can refuse to accept a parent who is a teen mother because you think she will be too difficult to handle. You can run a program that only accepts children of a certain age—you can decide not to accept infants or schoolagers on the basis of their age.

● ●

What to Say

If you decide not to enroll a child for any reason, the best thing to say is, "I don't think that this is the best place for your child at this time." If you try to explain yourself any further, you run the risk of saying something that might cause the parent to think you are practicing some kind of illegal discrimination. Many providers are tempted to say, "I'm full," or "I'm waiting to hear back from the family that I interviewed yesterday." However, it isn't a good idea to lie to parents. If you're caught lying (for example, if the parent sees a new ad for your program in the paper the following week), she may become angry and file a complaint.

● ●

Treat Everyone with Respect

You should treat *everyone* with respect and dignity. Just because you can discriminate against someone legally doesn't mean you should do so. If parents feel that they aren't being treated fairly, they are more likely to complain to your licensor, spread negative comments about your program, or sue you. This means that you shouldn't discriminate legally unless you have a very good reason to do so.

What are some situations in which you might want to discriminate legally?

- Some providers give discounts to low-income parents (where permissible) or to families who have more than one child enrolled.

- When some providers raise their rates, they only apply the higher rate to any new families who enroll.

- If a parent is experiencing a severe family hardship, you may decide not to charge the parent for a week or so until the emergency passes.

If you do treat parents differently, as in these examples, you should not try to hide the fact; eventually all the parents will probably find out. If you make it a policy to treat all parents the same way who are in the same situation, then you shouldn't have a problem. In other words, if you're asked by a parent why another family is getting special treatment, you can reply, "My policy is to briefly forgive some parent fees when a family has a serious emergency or hardship. If this happens to your family, I will give you the same consideration." However, don't put this policy in writing; you want to retain your flexibility in how you handle each unique situation.

A parent once called us with a complaint about her provider. After the parent terminated her contract, she found out that the provider was charging more to care for her infant than she was charging the other parents who had infants in her program. It appeared that the reason the provider was charging her more was because this parent picked up her child a half hour later than the other parents. However, the parent couldn't believe that this was the explanation for the higher rate. The extra fee seemed much too high to her. She believed that she was being charged more because she made more money than the other parents. We explained that it would have been perfectly legal for the provider to charge her more based on her income.

Whatever the reason for the higher fee, this provider should have done a better job of explaining her rate structure to this parent. By not doing so, she was increasing the likelihood of misunderstandings, complaints, and even lawsuits.

Screening New Families

A provider once called our office and said, "I just had an interview with a new parent last night. She was late for the interview, and when I asked her why, she said, 'I was meeting with my attorney to discuss suing my previous caregiver.'" The provider wanted to know if she could refuse to enroll this parent because of this statement. Since her reason for discriminating against the parent was not because the parent was in a protected class, the answer was yes.

You have the right to screen parents before enrolling them, and you may decide not to accept a family based on many reasons, including the fear of being sued. You can also refuse to provide care to any parent who seems to be asking too many questions about your insurance coverage. You can turn a parent down if you have any reason to believe that he or she will create legal problems for you or make frivolous complaints to your licensor.

In screening new families for your program, you should be sensitive to the same warning signs that you would consider when interviewing someone to be hired as an employee. To reduce your business risks, listen to what your intuition is telling you about prospective clients or employees.

Terminating a Contract

Just as you can legally refuse to enroll a parent in your program for many reasons (or even for no reason), you can also legally terminate your contract with a parent for many reasons. You might choose to terminate a family because you have a different philosophy of child rearing (the parent insists that you give the child homework every night, and you don't think that's reasonable), or for practical reasons (the parent's work schedule fluctuates, and you don't want to open your program an hour earlier on some days to accommodate her).

However, you need to be careful in how you handle a termination because there's always a possibility that the parent may feel angry or hurt, and this may lead them to take action against you (a complaint or lawsuit).

Don't write a letter to the parent explaining why you are terminating your contract—no matter what you write, the parent will see it as insulting and won't agree with your point of view. Furthermore, if you put your reasons in writing it's more likely that you'll unintentionally write something that will cause the parent to believe that you're practicing some kind of illegal discrimination. Instead, simply give the parent a statement that indicates the last day of care that you will provide for their child.

Ideally you will already have discussed the problems that led you to make the decision to terminate this family, and it's not a good idea to bring up those issues again, since you have made your decision. Inform your licensor about the termination and keep a record of all your dealings with this family in your own files, in case any problems arise later.

Discrimination Lawsuits Are Rare

Fortunately, few parents initiate discrimination lawsuits, because discrimination is quite difficult to prove. As long as you are treating your client parents with respect and keeping the lines of communication open, you shouldn't worry about the parents suing you for illegal discrimination. Use your contracts and policies as communication tools to help the parents understand your rules.

You should try to do everything that you can to remain respectful and cooperative with the parents in your program. As a rule, parents only sue when they feel that they have been mistreated by their provider. This means that there may be times when it will be best to let an insult or a strong opinion go unanswered, even if you know that you haven't done anything wrong. Defending yourself against a lawsuit can be very expensive and demoralizing, and any preventative action that you can take to head off a drawn-out legal battle will be well worth the effort.

Price Fixing

It's reasonable for family child care providers to want to know the fees that the other providers in their area are charging. And in trying to collect this information, you may have encountered one or more of the following situations:

- You move to a new town or neighborhood and call the other providers in the area to ask what they are charging parents for their programs.
- You participate in a discussion of what providers are charging at your monthly family child care association meeting.
- Your family child care association conducts a telephone survey of its members' rates for its parent referral service and shares the results at the next meeting.
- You go to a local child care center and explain, "I'm a family child care provider who lives a few blocks from here. Can I get a copy of your parent fee statement?"

However, there is a big problem here—in each of these scenarios you are probably violating state or federal price fixing laws. Federal antitrust law severely limits the ability of competitors to share information about their prices. In addition, your state may also have laws against price fixing. These laws are designed to encourage competition and to discourage competitors from setting their rates higher than they otherwise would. In all of the above situations family child care providers are sharing rate information, and this is likely to result in higher fees being charged to parents.

It's almost always illegal for competitors to share information about the rates that they are charging. It doesn't matter if the competitors don't come to any kind of formal agreement about their rates. There doesn't have to be an agreement to charge the same fees, or even to charge a fee within a specific range. Even an agreement to keep your fees stable is illegal.

For illegal price fixing to occur, both of the parties who are discussing the rates have to know that the other person is a competitor. So if you call up another provider and say, "I'm a family child care provider who's surveying other providers in my area to see what they're charging," this would be illegal under the above definition. However, if you call and say, "I'm surveying the family child care providers in the local area to see what they charge," this would probably be okay. In this case, you can't reveal that you are also a provider in the course of the telephone conversation.

It's probably also illegal to survey family child care providers about their rates if you are (and identify yourself as) a person who is thinking of becoming a provider but is not in business yet.

Whether you are in violation of the price fixing laws in any given situation will depend on the specific circumstance involved. However, we recommend that you be very cautious in discussing your rates with anyone.

Family child care associations that operate a referral service for parents can give specific rate information to any parents who call for a referral, but they can't share this information with the members of the association. This means that the person who surveys the members and collects their rates and the person who gives this information to the parents can't be providers who are competing with the members of the association. (They could be providers who live in another town or volunteers who aren't providers.)

How to Collect Rate Information

Having said all that, there are some legal ways that you can collect rate information about what other family child care providers are charging:

- Ask your local child care resource and referral agency if they have any rate information that they can share with you. Most agencies conduct rate surveys or can access this information. (Be sure to cooperate with any government agency that conducts a rate survey in your area.) Since the agency isn't your competitor, you can safely ask it for rate information, as long as the data was properly collected (see page 143). These agencies will usually share average rates by zip code or neighborhood. Ask if they can give you more specific information, such as the following:

  - The average rates for providers who have been in business roughly as long as you have (for example, less than two years, three to 10 years, or more than 10 years).
  - The average rates for providers who have similar characteristics (for example, NAFCC accreditation, CDA credential, larger program, infant-only program).
  - The average rates for a smaller area than your zip code.
  - The average rates for the child care centers in your area. (But be careful about using the average rates as a guide for setting your own rates. You aren't an "average" provider. If you're offering a high-quality program, you should charge above-average rates. For a discussion of how to set rates, see the *Family Child Care Marketing Guide*.)
  - Other fee information, such as vacation and sick day policies, paid holidays, late fees, registration fees, and so on.

- Look for any advertisements that list the rates of other family child care providers in your area (in newspaper or shopper ads, or on flyers posted on community bulletin boards or in local stores or businesses).

- When you interview prospective parents, ask about the child care fees and policies in their last program.

- When a parent leaves your program, ask about the child care fees and policies in their new program.

- You can go to a child care center and collect rate information legally as long as you don't reveal that you are a child care provider. It isn't a violation of the price fixing laws to ask a caregiver about prices if she doesn't know that you are a competitor.

Bear in mind that even if you collect rate information in one of these legal ways, you can't get together with other family child care providers and use this information to set your rates. You can share the information you have gathered, but you can't say, "Okay, now that we know what the average rates are in our neighborhood, let's all agree to make sure that our rates are above average."

●●●

How to Talk About Rates

What if a provider who is new to your area calls you and says, "I had my first interview last night, and I really like the family. I told them that I'd charge $20 per day, but I was real nervous when I discussed my rates. Do you think I'm charging too much, or is this not enough?" How should you respond to her?

You might say, "I'd be glad to discuss how you can become more comfortable when discussing your rates with parents, but we shouldn't be sharing specific information about our rates, because it's probably against the law. If you want to know what other providers charge, call your child care resource and referral agency. You could also have your husband call and ask other child care centers in this area what they charge. If your rates are less than what they charge, you shouldn't feel nervous about them. If your rates are higher, you could identify at least three things about your program that they don't offer (lower ratios, individually prepared meals, or more flexible hours) and promote these benefits to justify your fees."

●●●

Conducting a Rate Survey

If you belong to a family child care association (or any other organization) that wants to do a survey to collect child care rate data, your survey must meet all of the following tests in order to be legal:

- The survey must be conducted by an independent organization. For example, your association can hire a private consultant who is not a member of the association to do the survey.

- The sample of providers that you survey must be large enough that it would not be possible to identify the rates of any one provider.

- The information provided by the survey participants must be older than three months.

- The rate information that you gather must be presented in such a way that it would not be possible to identify the rates of any one provider.

- You must share the results of your survey with the public. You can do this by publishing the rate information that you have gathered in the local media or by distributing it through your local child care resource and referral agency or some other government agency.

Many family child care providers aren't aware of the price fixing laws, and they illegally share their rate information with other providers. In Minnesota, the state attorney general's office investigated a complaint that was made against a county family child care association that held a meeting in which the members' rates were discussed. In the end, the association officers signed an agreement with the state not to repeat this.

Although it's highly unlikely that two providers who privately discuss their rates will be prosecuted, you should remember that it is still probably illegal. By using the methods described above, you should be able to get the information that you need to find out if your rates are competitive. If you have any questions about how you can legally get or share price information, contact your state attorney general's office.

CHAPTER FOURTEEN

Barriers to Your Business

Chapter Summary
This chapter discusses how to handle the various types of business barriers that you
may encounter, whether in the form of housing barriers that attempt to prohibit your
business—or financial barriers, such as higher fees and taxes.

Are you allowed to care for children in your home or apartment? If you have fulfilled your
state's child care licensing requirements, or if you are exempt from them, this would seem to
be a simple question. But despite our society's purportedly deep concern for the welfare of
children, family child care providers continue to face many kinds of barriers to operating
their businesses. In some parts of the country these barriers can be a significant obstacle to
the very existence of family child care.

Housing Barriers
There are four major kinds of housing barriers that family child care providers may face:
restrictive zoning ordinances, prohibitions in rental leases, neighborhood opposition, and
deed restrictions on residential property. This chapter will focus primarily on the two most
common kinds of housing barriers—neighborhood opposition and deed restrictions—
because these are the issues that you are most likely to encounter.

Restrictive Zoning Ordinances
Your state, county, or city government may have established ordinances that restrict or discourage home-based businesses in residential areas. These ordinance may have conditional-
use permits that limit the number of children that you can care for. About one-fourth of the
states have state laws that say that family child care is permitted use in residential areas.
Where they exist, these state laws usually supersede any local government ordinances. But
in other parts of the country, local city and county zoning ordinances can create problems.
For information on how to work to change your state or local laws, see pages 154–55.

Rental Prohibitions
Some landlords of public and private apartments and houses refuse to allow their tenants to provide family child care in the rental units. The lease may bar any activity that isn't "residential use." For example, the lease of a Minneapolis apartment complex reads, "The Tenant shall use the premises only as a private dwelling for himself/herself . . ." The resident handbook is more specific: "A tenant cannot conduct business of any kind in their apartment or upon the premises." The best time to deal with these issues is before you sign or renew a lease, as described on pages 147–48.

Neighborhood Opposition
When you open a family child care business, your neighbors may become concerned about the effect that it will have on traffic, noise, or property values. They can bring these complaints to the police, the city council, or your licensing agency. (For an excellent publication on this topic, see *Landlord and Tenant Issues for Family Child Care,* which is listed in appendix B). This chapter provides several strategies for dealing with complaints from neighbors.

Deed Restrictions
The owners of residential property may adopt various deed restrictions in an effort to protect their property values. These restrictions, which are typically called covenants, conditions, and restrictions (CC&Rs), can be found in the bylaws and rules of homeowners associations, condominiums, housing cooperatives, townhouses, and even real estate developers. For example, a sample restrictive covenant from North Carolina reads, "All lots and lands shall be used exclusively for residential purposes." This chapter explains several strategies for dealing with this type of barrier.

• •

Family Child Care in Public Housing
If you live in federally subsidized public housing, you should be allowed to conduct your business without interference. Federal law doesn't prohibit family child care in public housing. Federal regulations allow tenants to "engage in legal profitmaking activities in the dwelling unit" where such activities are "incidental to the primary use of the leased unit for residence." Legal profitmaking activities are also permitted in Section 8 housing.

Housing and Urban Development officials have repeatedly interpreted federal regulations to permit family child care in federally subsidized public housing. If you live in public housing, are having problems with your landlord, and are not in violation of any local or state zoning ordinances, call the Child Care Law Center for assistance (see appendix B).

• •

Residential versus Business Restrictions

When you are facing a deed, lease, or zoning restriction of some kind, it will usually fall under one of two types of restrictions, residential or business:

- A residential restriction limits the property to residential use: "No part of the property shall be used for anything other than residential purposes."

- A business restriction prohibits any business or commercial use: "No unit shall be used for business or commercial purposes."

Although from a legal standpoint there may not be a major difference between these two types of restrictions, it can be helpful to distinguish between them in your arguments against a restriction:

- ***Residential use only:*** Family child care is residential use of a property in that it is using the space in exactly the same way that a large family would use it. If your state zoning laws allow family child care to be a permitted use in residential areas, you can argue that this supports your position.

- ***No business use:*** The authors of deed restrictions against businesses probably never considered family child care as a business. They simply wanted to exclude the homeowners from opening a printing shop in a basement or a pizza parlor in the living room. However, family child care is unlike virtually all other businesses, in that it requires no remodeling or special fixtures, plumbing, or electrical outlets.

Before You Buy or Lease

Before you buy or lease a home or apartment you should check to see if there are any restrictive zoning ordinances or deed or lease restrictions.

To find out if there are any zoning ordinances, contact your city or county clerk's office, your city attorney's office, or the local library. Sometimes there are zoning ordinances that prohibit family child care, but no one is paying attention to the rule. In doing your research you may want to use a low-key approach and not identify yourself, your address, or the type of business you want to start.

To find out if there are any deed or lease restrictions, look in the property title report or the bylaws (for a condominium or townhouse). Bear in mind that the restrictions may not be included directly in those documents; they may simply be referred to. Read the property title report or bylaws closely to see if it cites any other documents or rules that you may be bound by. Since your realtor and building inspector may not be aware of these restrictions, you may want to consult an attorney before signing any legal papers, to make sure that you can operate your business in this location.

What can you do if your homeowners association decides to change its policy about business restrictions after you have moved in? Check the association bylaws closely to see if they have followed their own procedures regarding policy changes. If not, you may be able to challenge the new, more restrictive policy on these grounds. Otherwise, you could try to gather enough votes to overturn the new rule.

You May Need Your Landlord's Permission

If you rent an apartment in some states, your licensing agency may require your landlord to give you written permission to operate a family child care business. Make sure that your landlord will sign this document before you sign a lease. Even if the lease doesn't exclude family child care, the landlord may have his own reasons for not signing.

If he refuses to give you permission, use the strategies described on pages 151–55 to try to overcome his objections. To address a landlord's concern that your business will create more wear and tear than a typical family, you can offer a larger security deposit, up to the legal maximum in your state. To allay any concerns about liability, list your landlord as an "additional insured" on your business liability policy (see page 68).

• •

Before You Sign a Lease
- Check to see if there are any restrictions against your business.
- Find out whether you or the landlord are responsible for compliance with the Americans with Disabilities Act (see page 135).
- If required by the licensing rules, get your landlord's permission to operate your business.
- If you have any questions, you may want to consult a lawyer.

Before You Buy a Home
- Check to see if there are any zoning or deed restrictions against operating your business.
- Find out if you must make the home accessible for persons with disabilities (see page 135).
- Be sure that you can get homeowners insurance (see page 80).
- If you have any questions, you may want to consult a lawyer.

• •

Prevent Problems by Being a Good Neighbor

The opposition to a family child care business usually comes from neighbors who contend that it will compromise the residential nature of the neighborhood, bring additional noise and traffic, lower the value of their property, or create liability risks. However, a well-run family child care business shouldn't create these kinds of problems for the neighbors, and often the real issues won't have much to do with your business, but will consist of more personal grievances.

Even if there is a deed restriction that prohibits your business, if no one complains about what you're doing you may never have a problem with it. In this kind of situation, it's extremely important to be a good neighbor and to handle any complaints quickly. If one of your children breaks a neighbor's window, or if a parent accidentally drives over a neighbor's lawn, approach the neighbor directly, apologize, and offer to make amends.

Even if you aren't operating under any restrictions, you need to try to be a good neighbor and work to allay your neighbors' fears about your business. Most of the opposition typically comes from ignorance about what it means to live near a family child care business. Personal contact with your closest neighbors can go a long way toward establishing goodwill in the neighborhood. Let your neighbors know how many children you will be caring for, what your daily routine will be like, and so on. Some providers have found it helpful to host an event, such as inviting the neighbors in for an afternoon snack or tea, to help them get to know the program.

Most important, you need to do whatever you can to minimize the negative effects of your business on the neighborhood. This means that you should tell parents not to block the neighbors' driveways, turn around in them, or double park while dropping off or picking up their children. Make sure that the children in your care don't run across your neighbors' lawns or ride their bikes across your neighbors' driveways, and so on.

(The above information is adapted from *Deed Restrictions as Impediments to Family Day Care: The Problem and Potential Solutions*, published by the Child Care Law Center. This publication is not listed in appendix B because it is out of print.)

● ●

Explain the Benefits of a Family Child Care Business
To counter any complaints about your family child care business, you can promote some of its positive aspects. You can argue that your neighborhood is safer because you are at home all day keeping an eye out for trouble while the neighbors are at work. The service that you provide to parents helps them keep their jobs and adds stability to the neighborhood. Your business may even attract new tenants or buyers to the area. If you care for children who live close to your home, this cuts down on the parents' transportation time and actually reduces traffic.

● ●

If You Have Complaints about Your Neighbors
There may also be situations when your neighbors will cause you to be concerned. For example:

● A neighbor's dog may enter your yard while the children in your care are playing outside.
● A neighbor may have a pool that isn't enclosed by a fence.
● The neighborhood teenagers may race their cars past your home.

When you have a problem, you should talk with your neighbors about how the situation creates a safety concern for the children in your care, and try to come to a reasonable compromise about it. If a neighbor is uncooperative or hostile, contact your licensor immediately, and ask her to make a note about the conversation in your files. This will help to protect you if the unhappy neighbor later makes a complaint against you to the licensing agency.

● ●

Notify Your Licensor

If someone is trying to enforce a deed restriction against you or a neighbor is complaining about your business, they may also file a complaint against you with your licensor. It may be a minor complaint ("the children are making noise when they play outside") or a major one ("she leaves the children outside unattended for hours").

Even if the complaint is baseless, you need to protect yourself against this possibility. One way to do this is to stay in regular contact with your licensor and tell her what is happening, so that there will be a record of the situation in your files. If necessary, write a letter to your licensor summarizing the events that have occurred.

Keeping your licensor informed can help to blunt any unfounded complaints. If the licensor knows your situation, it will be much easier for her to recognize baseless complaints or to give you the benefit of the doubt when it's another person's word against yours.

● ●

The Case of the "24-Hour Care" Sign

A provider in St. Paul provided 24-hour child care in her federally subsidized home for over six months without incident. Then her enrollment dropped, and she placed a sign on her front lawn advertising her 24-hour child care. Her next-door neighbor immediately started complaining about the noise of children playing outside and car doors slamming late at night.

The neighbor hired a lawyer and asked the provider to remove the sign and close her business. The provider discovered that there was a local ordinance against large signs in the neighborhood, so she replaced her sign with a smaller one. (Don't put up a sign in front of your home without finding out whether the local laws permit this, and if they do, whether they regulate the size and location of the sign.)

The provider continued to make other efforts to address her neighbor's concerns, but he refused to be reasonable. Instead, he filed complaints with the provider's licensing agency, the federal housing agency that owned the property, and the city zoning department. The licensing agency responded that the provider was in compliance with all their rules, and the housing agency responded that she was in compliance with her lease with them. The zoning department didn't take any action because Minnesota has a state zoning law that allows family child care to operate in residential neighborhoods.

However, instead of giving up, the neighbor brought his complaint before the St. Paul city council and asked them to force her to stop offering care in the evening. She had to present her side of the case to the city council. We helped her get through this ordeal and spoke on her behalf. The council decided not to intervene in the matter, referring it to a mediator instead. We tried to reach an agreement with the neighbor in the mediation meeting, but he continued to be unreasonable, and it ended without any resolution. In the end, there was nothing that he could do, and the provider continued to offer 24-hour child care.

There were several reasons why this provider was able to succeed against a determined adversary—she wasn't in violation of any state or local laws, she did everything that she could to reasonably accommodate the neighbor's concerns, she sought outside help to write letters and speak in her defense, and she stood her ground and refused to back down.

Strategies for Dealing with Housing Barriers

If your neighbors complain about your business or try to use a deed restriction against you, there are six strategies that you can use to defend yourself:

- Get a copy of the restriction.
- Keep a written record.
- Define the problem (noise, traffic, liability, property values).
- Make an appeal and get support for your case.
- Get legal help.
- Change the law.

Get a Copy of the Restriction

When someone says that you can't operate your business, your first response should be, "Where does it say that?" Get a copy of the ordinance or deed restriction and examine it closely to see if it really does apply to you. This is too important for you to take anyone else's word about it. The restriction may actually be against child care centers, not family child care, it may only limit the number of children who are in care, or the rule may be unclear. You may want to ask an attorney to read the restriction and advise you whether it applies to your situation.

Keep a Written Record

It's important to keep written records of the process of defending yourself. Use a notebook to keep a chronological journal of events. Record a summary of every conversation that you have with the complaining neighbor, the representatives of the homeowners association, the lawyers involved in the case, and so on. Make particular note of any language that other people use that promises something or is abusive or threatening; you may be able to use this against them later. Keep copies of any letters or documents that you receive and pay attention to any deadlines contained in them. A complete record of the process is useful in helping you remember what others said and did, and when. It will also be helpful to your attorney, if you choose to hire one.

Define the Problem

Deed restrictions were originally designed to ensure that homeowners would be able to enjoy their property without disruption. When someone tries to use a deed restriction against you, you should ask, "What is the specific problem that my business is creating that the restriction is designed to prevent?" Your goal is to argue that there really isn't any problem, and that you should be able to operate your business. Complaints from neighbors usually involve noise, traffic, liability, or property values. Let's examine each of these areas in turn.

Noise

It's reasonable to expect a lower level of noise on a residential street than in a commercial area. However, you can argue that the noise made by the children in your care is hardly the same as the noise from a factory or a neighborhood bar. In fact, it's probably about the same noise that a large family might make. Ask the neighbors about their specific concerns and ask for a chance to address them. You may be able to address complaints about specific kinds of noises by any of these:

- Ask parents not to honk their horns or slam their car doors.
- Close the windows of your home when the children are playing inside.
- Consider your neighbor's concerns when scheduling outdoor activities with the children.

If you think that the complaints have been exaggerated, you could ask your homeowners association to monitor the noise from your business for a trial month.

Some neighbors who complain about noise may actually be concerned that your business will be open at all hours of the day or night. To help allay these concerns, you can give them a copy of your schedule or show them any licensing rules that limit the time that the children are in your home.

Traffic

Neighbors who make complaints about traffic are sometimes confusing a family child care business with a child care center. They imagine that dozens of cars will be coming and going each day, rather than the four or five cars that you are likely to have. Explain to your neighbors how many cars drive up to your home each day. If there is a specific problem with the traffic, such as parents blocking a driveway or driving too fast, ask for time to address these concerns with the parents who are involved. It's hard to imagine that traffic problems would be a real concern to any reasonable person who understands your business.

Liability

When people imagine children playing outside or in the public areas in an apartment, condominium, or residences that belong to a homeowners association, they often express concern about who will be held liable if there is an accident. Everyone is afraid of a lawsuit, and this fear is aggravated when children are involved. Although you can certainly explain how hard you work to protect the children, the most practical response to this concern is to buy adequate business liability coverage and list your landlord or homeowners association as an "additional insured."

The extra cost associated with adding these names should be minimal, and it means that these people will be insured against any of the cost of defending themselves in any lawsuit that arises from an incident with the children in your care and any money damages that are awarded.

Show your landlord or homeowners association a copy of your license or state registration certificate. Explain to them that your compliance with health and safety rules probably exceeds what most of the families in the neighborhood are doing to protect their children. Encourage them to contact your licensor for more information. Use your compliance with the regulations to show that you are doing everything possible to reduce the liability risks associated with your business.

Property Values

Do property values decline when there is a family child care provider in the neighborhood? Although some people may think that they do, there's no evidence of this. If someone alleges that your business will cause local property values to drop, ask to see the records that support this claim; you will find that they don't exist, for two reasons. First, it's virtually impossible to track the effect of a family child care business on the property sales in a neighborhood. Second, the truth may be just the opposite. Families who are looking for a new home may find a neighborhood more attractive if there is quality child care close by. If the families of the children in your care live in your housing project building or homeowners association, point this out to show that you are actually providing a valuable service that only increases the appeal of your neighborhood.

Make an Appeal and Get Support for Your Case

When a deed restriction is used against you, find out if there's any way to appeal it. If your landlord says that your lease prohibits your business, ask to talk with the management company, owner, or whoever has the power to change the lease. If you're challenged by your homeowners, condominium, or cooperative association, ask to appear before the board or governing body. You want to argue your case with those in charge. You may be able to convince them to grant you a waiver, give you time to find a solution, or change the restriction.

Usually you have nothing to lose by fighting back—and sometimes if you make enough noise, you can win. In general, the more publicity you generate about your case, the better. Ask your local family child care association, licensor, and child care resource and referral agency for support. They may be able to write letters on your behalf or appear at meetings.

Talk to all your neighbors and ask for their support by signing a petition, attending a meeting, or contacting those in authority. You'll probably find that there are neighbors who are operating other kinds of home businesses, and you can make the argument that if one type of business is restricted, then all businesses may be. You should be able to generate support by arguing that all home businesses should stand together and fight for a change in the restrictions.

Call your local newspaper and television station, and ask them to report the story. The public will probably be very supportive. You may be able to describe yourself as a small businessperson, a mother formerly on welfare, a woman caring for children from low-income families who are moving off welfare, a family caring for special-needs children, or a program that is offering quality care for neighborhood children. These kinds of descriptions will attract sympathy and support, and may bring powerful public pressure on the decision-makers to resolve the case in your favor.

If there is one person in particular who is complaining about your business, it may be appropriate to suggest that you and this person meet with a mediator to resolve the problem. Many communities have mediation services that try to help disputing parties come to a reasonable resolution of their problems. The cost of a mediation service is usually very low, and just making the offer to use a mediator can help you to win over more support. (To find out if there is a mediation service in your community, contact your local branch of the United Way.)

Get Legal Help

If you can afford it, hire a lawyer to argue your case. A lawyer can research state law to see if there are similar cases that were decided favorably for you. She can also write letters, talk to officials, appear at meetings, and speak on your behalf. Sometimes just having a lawyer on your side will cause your opponents to take your case more seriously or even back off. If you can't afford a lawyer to argue for you, you may still want to hire a lawyer to do specific services, such as preliminary research to see if you have a legitimate legal defense.

Call your county bar association for referrals to lawyers. Some bar associations have lawyers who work pro bono (without charge) for certain types of cases for lower-income clients. You could also contact a local Legal Aid office. For more information about finding a lawyer, see chapter 15.

Change the Law

The final strategy is to try to change the law in your favor. This should be your last resort after all the other strategies have failed, since it's a long, difficult process and may not be completed in time to affect your case. However, it is a way that you can make a difference that will help other family child care providers.

Changing Your Local Laws or Regulations

To change a city or county zoning ordinance, approach your local representative (council-person or county commissioner) and ask for help. Explain why the law wasn't designed for your particular business or how your business is a benefit to the community (particularly if you are caring for the children of low-income families). Use the strategies given in this chapter to argue why your business doesn't cause the problems that other businesses do.

Since elected officials respond to public pressure, the key to your success may be the support network that you developed in appealing your case—your family child care association, licensor, parents, sympathetic neighbors, the media. Present your case to as many people as possible and urge them to contact the elected officials involved.

Changing Your State Law
There are no federal laws that supersede state and local laws and require them to permit family child care businesses. This means that each state can enforce its own laws, and what is permitted in one state may be outlawed in another. Zoning ordinances are set and controlled at the state and local level. Deed restrictions are private agreements that aren't usually controlled by the state or local government.

However, the enforcement of deed restrictions can be limited by state law, and the best way to eliminate housing barriers to family child care is to enact a state law that prevents local governments from imposing restrictive zoning ordinances or landlords and homeowners associations from using deed restrictions. California has such a law; it reads:

> Every restriction or prohibition entered into, whether by way of covenant, condition upon use or occupancy, or upon transfer of title to real property, which restricts or prohibits directly, or indirectly limits, the acquisition, use or occupancy of such property for a family day care home for children is void (California Health and Safety Code Section 1597.40 (c)).

The Child Care Law Center in California has done a lot of work in this area, and if you are considering trying to make a change to your state law, you should contact them. (See appendix B for contact information.)

Financial Barriers

In addition to the housing barriers that attempt to shut down your family child care business, you may also encounter financial barriers that simply want to make money from your business. These barriers include special fees and taxes, higher utility rates, commercial rates, and "no commercial use" clauses in warranties. Many of these barriers are unfair or based on a misunderstanding of your business. However, in many cases there are ways that you can challenge or change them.

Special Fees

In an effort to increase their revenues, some city and county governments have imposed special fees on family child care providers, such as licensing fees and fees for building and fire inspections. (If you pay these fees, bear in mind that they are 100% deductible on your federal tax returns.)

However, if you are charged special fees, you could argue that you are being discriminated against unless similar fees are imposed on all family child care providers, including unregulated, exempt, and even illegal providers. You could also argue that the tax is discriminatory unless it's being enforced consistently against all home-based businesses. The more businesses that a tax affects, the more supporters you will be able to draw on to fight it.

Tangible Personal Property Taxes

Some cities impose a tangible personal property tax on the equipment used in home-based businesses in order to raise additional revenue. The tax can apply to the furniture and appliances used by family child care providers. Before you pay a tax of this kind, look closely at the law and ask yourself these questions:

- Does the tax apply to family child care businesses, or just child care centers?
- Does the tax apply only to items used 100% in a business? If it does apply to items that are used for both business and personal purposes, it's probably based only on the business portion of the item, which will usually be your Time-Space percentage. (For more information, see the *Record-Keeping Guide*.)
- Does the tax apply only to newly purchased equipment?
- Does the tax apply to items that have been fully depreciated?

You can also ask a city official for clarification; however, before you accept the answers that you receive, you may want to contact your elected representative and ask if she thinks that this law applies to you. And, as above, you could also argue that the tax shouldn't be applied to you unless it's enforced consistently against all home-based businesses, including unregulated, exempt, and illegal child care providers.

Higher Utility Rates

Some local governments also attempt to charge family child care providers higher rates for utilities, such as water, garbage, and sewer. These rate increases are usually justified by claiming that since you are running a business you should be charged a "commercial" rate. To fight these fees you could use the strategies for handling housing barriers outlined earlier in this chapter, as well as the following approaches:

- Find out whether the definition of "commercial use" in the law applies to family child care. A close reading of the law may find that it is meant to cover child care centers, not homes. If state zoning laws permit family child care in residential areas, you can argue that it's really not commercial use. If you aren't required to buy a city or county business license, then you can assert that you shouldn't be treated as a commercial business, since commercial businesses must purchase commercial licenses.

- The reason that commercial businesses are charged higher fees for utilities is because they use them at a higher rate. However, you can bet that no one in your local government has any evidence that shows that providers use utilities at a higher rate than regular families. Some providers can argue that they actually generate less garbage because they recycle or the children they care for are infants and they use a diaper service. It may help to educate local officials about what a family child care business is really like.

• The higher utility fees probably aren't being applied to other home-based businesses, or even to all child care providers in your area. For example, are computer programmers, artists, and Tupperware consultants also paying higher fees? What about unregulated and illegal child care providers? Is the fee based on your licensed capacity or your enrollment? If you're charged more for using more garbage, are the parents being charged less for using less? You could assert that you're being discriminated against, and your local officials may back off if they think that enforcing the ordinance will open a can of worms.

Commercial Rates

Some companies charge higher "commercial" rates to business customers. For example, some telephone companies will charge you a commercial rate if you use your phone number in any advertising (business cards, flyers, Yellow Pages ads).

Some years ago we approached our regional telephone company, and asked them to change their policy of charging a commercial rate to child care providers. We explained what a family child care business was and argued that the commercial rate was not appropriate for this type of business—and they agreed to make the change. You could work with your local association to lobby your telephone company in the same way.

"No Commercial Use" Clauses

Before you buy any major appliances—such as a refrigerator, freezer, dishwasher, washer, or dryer—read the warranty and extended warranty closely. If there is a "no commercial use" clause, ask for clarification and a written statement that this clause doesn't apply to your business before you buy.

We know of a provider who was accused of violating the "no commercial use" clause of the warranty on her dishwasher because she had used it in her child care business. In this case she was able to successfully argue that her use of the dishwasher shouldn't be treated any differently from a normal household. However, to avoid problems it's best to handle this issue before you buy.

Working with a Lawyer

Chapter Summary
This chapter discusses when you need to consult a lawyer and how to find and work with a lawyer.

Most of us have little, if any, contact with lawyers, and we're usually glad that this is the case. However, lawyers can help you avoid problems by advising you how to reduce the risks of lawsuits or criminal charges. In addition, lawyers can defend you if you are sued or face criminal prosecution.

When You Should Consult a Lawyer

You might anticipate that if you ever end up working with a lawyer, it would mean that you're in serious trouble and that it will cost you a lot of money. However, this isn't necessarily the case. There are actually two kinds of situations in which you should be working with a lawyer, and only one is when you are trying to keep yourself or a family member from going to jail. The other situation is when you are trying to to protect your assets.

Protect Your Assets

Here are some of the kinds of circumstances in which you might want to consider calling upon a lawyer to protect your assets and prevent trouble:

- When you are considering establishing a partnership or incorporating your business, a lawyer can draft your articles of incorporation and bylaws and advise you about how to protect your assets and limit your liability. We strongly recommend consulting an attorney and tax professional in this situation.

- When you write up your contract, a lawyer can review it to make sure the language that you are using clearly reflects your intentions and is likely to stand up in court.

- Before you sign a lease, a lawyer can review it to protect your rights and to ensure that you will be able to run your business at that location.

- Before you buy or rent property a lawyer can review any deed restrictions, homeowner association covenants, or zoning ordinances, research the laws in your state that may restrict your business, and advise you whether you should proceed. She can also represent you if you are fighting any of these kinds of restrictions by attending hearings or writing letters on your behalf.

- When you hire employees, a lawyer can advise you about setting up your personnel policies and employee benefits or clarify your rights as an employer.

- When a parent leaves owing you money, a lawyer may be able to help you collect the money by writing a letter or representing you in small claims court.

- If you (or a family member) are injured or your property is destroyed because of someone else's negligence, a lawyer can help you.

Stay Out of Trouble

There are also situations where someone else is threatening to take away your assets, your license to run your business, or your freedom. Here are some of these circumstances in which you should consult an attorney to defend you:

- A parent sues you for an injury to their child or themselves.

- Your licensing worker is taking action against you that may result in your license being suspended or revoked.

- The police or child protective services open an investigation against you or another family member because of a criminal complaint of child abuse or neglect.

- An employee sues you for violating her rights or for an injury that she suffered while working for you.

- You receive an audit notice from the IRS. (You may also hire an enrolled agent [EA] or certified public accountant [CPA] to represent you in an audit. For more information, see the *Family Child Care Audit Manual*.)

- A parent sues or countersues you in small claims court. Usually a lawyer isn't used in small claims court, but if the amount of money involved is important to you, it may be worth considering. (Some states will prohibit you from being represented by a lawyer in small claims court, but in that case it might still be helpful to consult a lawyer.)

If a Parent Threatens to Sue You

Although this book gives many examples of lawsuits that were brought by parents against their family child care provider, these cases really aren't that common. A parent may threaten to sue you in order to intimidate you, but few will actually follow through because of the cost and time involved.

If a parent says to you, "I'm going to sue you!" or "I'll see you in court!" your best response is to do nothing. In most cases nothing will happen after everyone has a chance to cool down. Don't threaten to sue the parent in return, because this may motivate the parent to consult a lawyer or to sue you when they might otherwise have let the matter drop.

The Kinds of Legal Actions

Here are four kinds of legal actions that might be taken against a family child care provider:

- A licensing complaint
- An IRS audit
- A civil lawsuit where money damages are being sought
- A criminal complaint by the police where the consequences are jail time

For information about handling a licensing complaint, see pages 20–22. For information about handling an audit, see the *Family Child Care Audit Manual*. You will find out that a civil lawsuit has been initiated against you when you receive a copy of a written complaint from the court system. It will give the name of the party who is suing you and the financial damages that they are seeking to recover. If this happens, you should consider contacting an attorney without delay.

You will find out that there is a criminal complaint against you when you are arrested by the police. You may not want to wait until this happens to hire an attorney. If you know that you are under investigation by the police or child protection services you should seek the advice of legal counsel.

● ●

Using a Mediation Service

One way to avoid a lawsuit is to use a mediation service. Mediation services bring both sides together and try to resolve the problem through informal discussions. Both sides must voluntarily agree to seek help from a mediator, and any agreement that is reached cannot be enforced by a court. Mediation services are usually very inexpensive (less than $100). To find out if a mediation service in available in your area, contact your local United Way or look in the Yellow Pages.

● ●

What to Do Before You Hire a Lawyer

There are some things that you can do to protect your interests before you consult an attorney. As described in chapters 4 and 6, it's important to keep regular notes about any illnesses, injuries, or problem behavior by a child, any outbursts or complaints by a parent, and any conflicts with the families in your care. Also, when any of these situations arise, always contact your licensor and ask her for advice about how to defuse any hard feelings that are brewing.

If you're having a serious conflict with an unhappy parent, you may also want to contact your business liability insurance agent even before you're sued. She may be able to advise you about what kinds of records to keep and how to proceed.

If you're sued, make a note of the deadline by which you must respond. If you miss any court deadlines you can substantially impair your ability to win your case. Notify your business liability insurance company immediately that you have been sued. One of the primary reasons for buying business liability insurance is for legal protection against lawsuits, and you want to take advantage of your benefits and seek legal assistance as soon as possible.

If you're sued, don't alter any of your records, and don't talk with anyone else about the case, especially the person who is suing you. If you are contacted by the opposing party or her attorney, don't discuss your case, whether or not you have already hired a lawyer. The party who is suing you is not your friend, and you shouldn't make any attempt to try to clear up the matter directly. To protect your interests, get an attorney. Tell her what happened and follow her instructions about how to proceed.

How to Find a Lawyer

Hiring a lawyer can be expensive. Although some legal fees are based on a flat rate for specific services, most rates are charged by the hour and they may range from $75 to $200 per hour or more In some cases you may be able to negotiate a legal fee up front. (The costs of all legal expenses for your business are 100% tax deductible.) To find out the range of the lawyers' fees in your area, contact your state bar association. Before you hire a lawyer you should explore whether there's any way to get legal representation at little or no cost to you. For example, explore the following options:

- Does your business liability insurance, car insurance, homeowners insurance, renter's insurance, or umbrella liability insurance have coverage for legal defense?

- Will anyone else's insurance pay for your attorney fees? (If a child was injured at a mall or on a swing set in the playground of your apartment complex, and you are sued by the parent, find out if the insurance company for the mall or the landlord will pay your legal fees.)

- Is Legal Aid (also called Legal Services) able to provide you with free legal assistance? (Legal Aid is a government program that represents low-income families. To find out if you qualify for this service, look for Legal Aid in the Yellow Pages or contact your local United Way.)

- If you believe that you are being discriminated against based on race, sex, religion, or disability, you may be able to get legal assistance from a public interest legal organization at a low cost. (These organizations include the ACLU, the NAACP Legal Defense Fund, the Lambda Legal Defense and Education [for gay and lesbian rights], and the National Women's Law Center.)

- Some lawyers offer their services pro bono (without charging) as a service to their community. Ask your local Legal Aid office or your local county bar association for the names of lawyers who might help you.

- If you live in a city that has a law school, you may be able to get free assistance if the school sponsors law clinics. These clinics, supervised by law professors, are designed to provide law students with real case experiences. The law students can do research, write letters, and represent you in some situations. These clinics are usually only available to low-income individuals and the school may have other guidelines for which cases they will handle. Contact any law school in your area and ask if they have a clinic. If they don't, ask if they can refer you to attorneys who may be able to help you.

- If you are facing criminal charges and have a low income, you may be eligible to have a public defender who will represent you for free. The police will give you information about this service.

- One way to afford legal protection is to buy legal insurance through a private company, such as Pre-Paid Legal Services. If you join this plan you will pay a monthly fee and receive legal assistance either at no charge or at a significant discount. The services offered include telephone consultation, contract review, audit help, civil and criminal law defense, will preparation, and more. Before enrolling, carefully consider whether your use of the service will justify its cost. For more information, contact Pre-Paid Legal Services at 321 East Main Street, Ada, Oklahoma 74820 (800-654-7757; www.prepaidlegal.com).

- The following organizations may also be able to refer you to a lawyer you can afford: the local county bar association, the local tenant's association, the Small Business Development Association, the National Association for the Self-Employed, the American Association of Retired People, and the United Way.

• •

The Child Care Law Center

The Child Care Law Center is a "nonprofit legal services organization that uses legal tools to make high quality, affordable child care available to every child, every family, and every community." They have done excellent work on deed restrictions and zoning ordinances, the Americans with Disabilities Act, custody and child abuse issues, liability, and other legal issues that affect family child care providers.

The center operates an information and referral line that is open a few afternoons per week. (See their Web site or call them for their current schedule.) They can answer legal questions on the phone and they may also be able to refer you to other legal professionals. They also have several helpful publications. For contact information, see the listing for the Child Care Law Center in appendix B.

• •

If none of the above resources can help you, you will need to hire a lawyer yourself. Start by asking other people for the names of lawyers who they would recommend. Talk to your relatives, friends, other providers, your tax preparer, insurance agents, the parents of the children in your care, and your local child care resource and referral agency. Your town may have a legal referral service that is sponsored by the state or county bar association. Look in the Yellow Pages under "Attorney Referral." (Use these referral services with caution; they don't evaluate the skill or experience of the attorneys when they provide a referral.)

Most lawyers specialize in a particular type of law, and you will make the best use of a lawyer's skills if you hire an attorney who has experience with the legal area that you are dealing with. If you want someone to incorporate your business, look for someone who has experience setting up small businesses. If the licensing agency wants to revoke your license, find a lawyer who specializes in administrative law. If you are arrested, you will need a criminal lawyer.

Don't simply hire the first lawyer you are referred to. Shop around and try to talk with at least three lawyers before you make a decision. Ask each one about their experience with the kind of legal problem that you are facing. Ask for an initial consultation to review the facts of your case. Many lawyers won't charge for an initial half-hour discussion. Use this time to help you choose the right lawyer for your situation by asking the following questions:

- How many other cases like mine have you handled?
- What do you charge? Are there additional charges for filing fees, copying, secretarial services, other?
- How many hours do you think it will take to resolve my problem?
- How long will it take you to return my calls?

Choosing a lawyer is a personal matter. You want to find someone you trust and who will be accessible to you. If you don't trust your lawyer you probably won't follow her advice, and then you'll have paid her for nothing. Don't base your decision only on which lawyer charges the least. A higher-priced attorney who has a great deal of experience with your kind of problem may be able to handle the case faster than an inexperienced lawyer who charges less per hour. Trust your instincts, and look for someone who is compatible with you and with whom you can establish a personal rapport.

How to Work with a Lawyer

Once you have chosen a lawyer, ask her to draw up a written agreement that spells out how much you will be charged, when you will be billed, and what she will do for you. Also, show her your insurance policies so that she can decide if your insurance company was correct in saying that it didn't have to cover your attorney's fees.

You can keep your legal fees lower if you use your lawyer's time effectively. Prepare for meetings by bringing all the documents that you were asked to provide and by writing down your questions beforehand. Ask your lawyer if you can collect any additional information yourself and request that she send you copies of any letters or documents that she sends to someone else. This will allow you to stay current with the progress of your case without having to pay for your lawyer's time to explain what she has done.

When it comes time to make a decision about your case, ask your lawyer what she recommends and why. She should present you with several options and describe the advantages and disadvantages of each option. If you have chosen your lawyer carefully, you should feel comfortable with her recommendation. However, don't feel that you have to rush into making a decision in your lawyer's office. Go home and take all the time that you need before you decide how to proceed.

(For more information, consult the Child Care Law Center publications on hiring a lawyer and locating legal services listed in appendix B.)

PART IV

Choosing a Business Structure

CHAPTER SIXTEEN

Business Structure Options

Chapter Summary
This chapter introduces the four business entities that you can choose for your family child care business. It explains which structure is best for most providers and how to tell if you should consider a different business structure.

Choosing a business structure is an important decision. Most family child care providers set themselves up as a self-employed sole proprietor without much thought. However, the three other kinds of business entities (general partnerships, limited liability companies, and corporations) are getting more attention, and it's important to understand the differences between them. Otherwise, you won't be able to make an informed choice about which structure is best in your situation.

● ●

Get Professional Help
This chapter outlines the key differences between the various business structures. However, this is a complex topic that is subject to different state rules and federal tax laws, and you shouldn't make a decision based only on the information given here. If you're setting up any business entity other than a sole proprietorship, you should consult a lawyer and a tax professional who are experienced with that entity.

For tax help, consider hiring an enrolled agent (EA) or a certified public accountant (CPA). These are tax professionals who have passed tests and must meet continuing education requirements. For help with federal and state payroll tax forms, consider hiring a payroll service or an accountant. Getting professional advice up front can pay off by saving you time and money later on.

● ●

The Four Business Entities

There are basically four kinds of business entities that you can choose for your business: a sole proprietorship, a partnership, a limited liability company, and a corporation.

Sole Proprietorship

A sole proprietorship consists of a self-employed person who runs a one-person business. The sole proprietor keeps all the profit, makes all the decisions, and can be held personally liable for anything that occurs in the business. A sole proprietor faces less regulation than any of the other business entities.

Partnership

A general partnership is an unincorporated business of two or more people who run the business and share the profit and loss. In family child care there are usually just two partners—a mother and daughter, a husband and wife, or two caregivers. A partnership is more complex to operate than a sole proprietorship, and it doesn't offer any limitations on your personal liability. In addition, some state regulations have restrictions on partnerships in family child care. (See page 171 for a description of a limited liability partnership.)

Limited Liability Company (LLC)

An LLC is a relatively new kind of business entity that offers the limited personal liability of a corporation without the complex paperwork requirements. From a tax perspective, it is treated the same way as a sole proprietor. You can set up a one-person LLC, a partnership LLC, or a corporate LLC. We will primarily discuss the option of a one-person LLC. A partnership LLC follows the requirements of a partnership and a corporate LLC follows the requirements of a corporation. Your state laws will have specific rules about LLCs, but only Massachusetts and the District of Columbia don't allow one-person LLCs.

Corporation

A corporation is a legal entity that is owned by its shareholders. Although this option offers limited personal liability and some tax advantages, it requires you to maintain precise business records and to observe many business formalities. (See page 183 for an explanation of the differences between an S and a C corporation.)

● ●

Get Licensed First

In most states you have to meet the licensing requirements before you can form any business entity other than a sole proprietorship. Since the state regulations for business entities vary, before you decide to set up a general partnership, LLC, or corporation, you should ask your secretary of state's office for the rules in your state.

● ●

About Partnerships

If you're considering setting up a partnership with another provider, it's important to understand the various kinds of partnership options and the issues that are involved with each of them.

Limited Liability Partnerships

So far, we have been describing general partnerships. However, there's another type of partnership, called a limited liability partnership, that consists of at least one general partner and one limited partner. The general partner has the same liability exposure as the partners in a general partnership. The limited partner has limited liability, but can't participate in the management of the business. Since it seems unlikely that a family child care provider would want to be a limited partner, this book will only discuss general partnerships.

Informal Partnerships

Let's say that you start a business with another caregiver and work together as partners. You share the parent income and business expenses and make all your business decisions together. However, you each file your own federal tax forms as a sole proprietor. Is your business a partnership? No. In order to become a partnership, you have to register a written partnership agreement with your state and file partnership tax forms (see pages 178 and 182).

It isn't clear how the IRS would treat this kind of informal business arrangement. It might say that one partner is the employee of the other, or could consider your business to be a partnership for tax purposes only. Either way, you and your partner would have filed your taxes improperly.

There are also potential liability problems in operating an informal partnership. If a problem arises, you could both be sued, and you would face a liability risk unless you both have adequate business liability insurance. If only one partner is insured, she could try to argue that the other partner is really an employee and should be covered by her policy. (If only one of you is insured, be sure to add the other partner's name as an additional insured, although she may also be covered as an employee.)

Spousal Partnerships

If you work with your husband doing child care, you don't have to form a partnership. You can be a sole proprietor and pay your husband for his work, or your husband can work for your business without pay. You shouldn't form a partnership with your spouse unless you feel strongly that you want to be recognized in business as equal partners.

If both you and your spouse want to show income on your tax returns toward your individual Social Security accounts, you must either form a partnership or have one spouse employ the other. You aren't allowed to simply divide up your income at the end of the year and file two **Schedule C** tax forms.

Two Businesses in One Home

Instead of establishing a formal partnership, two providers could run two separate businesses out of one home. Each provider would need to have separate clients and separate contracts with her clients. The businesses would need to keep completely separate records, and the providers would need to file separate tax forms. Only the provider who owns the home could deduct house expenses on **Form 8829.** If one provider pays rent, she could deduct this on her **Schedule C** and the homeowner would report this rental income on **Schedule E.** However, the homeowner wouldn't be able to claim the same amount of home deductions as a self-employed person (see page 182).

This kind of arrangement usually doesn't work out, because the providers tend to end up operating as one business, and it can be difficult to divide the income and expenses between them. There may also be licensing or Food Program restrictions to consider (check with your licensor and your Food Program sponsor). For example, the licensing rules may require that you be licensed separately for two different groups of children.

Financial Considerations of a Partnership

Since you must split the income from a partnership, it doesn't make financial sense to form a partnership unless the income of the partnership will be a lot bigger than your income as a sole proprietor. In other words, if you have been making a $20,000 profit as a sole proprietor and decide to form a partnership with the profit split 50-50, the total profit of the business would have to double for you to make the same amount you were making before. (The most likely way to do this would be to double the number of children in the program.) If the partners are family members, such as a husband and wife, or a wife and daughter, it may not be as important to increase the business profit by as much.

What about a Nonprofit Corporation?

A nonprofit (or "tax-exempt") corporation is a legal entity that's intended to benefit the public, rather than its shareholders. This wouldn't be suitable if you want to charge fees for your services and keep the profit that you make. Also, if you form a nonprofit corporation, you will be hired as its employee, and you won't have any Social Security tax savings.

Providers who are considering establishing a nonprofit corporation usually do so because they want to receive charitable contributions from corporations or individuals. They believe that this would be a good way to get funds to help them operate their business. However, qualifying for tax-exempt status is difficult and requires approval from your state as well as the IRS. It's unlikely that the IRS will approve you as a tax-exempt organization unless you can show that you are offering a community service that reaches more than just a handful of children.

If you decide to seek tax-exempt status, you should first consult an attorney and a tax professional. Bear in mind that nonprofit corporations must register with their state, follow the relevant state laws, and observe most of the same business formalities as other corporations. They must also make their federal tax returns available to the public when requested.

How to Choose a Business Entity

When family child care providers consider a business entity other than a sole proprietorship, it is usually for one or two primary reasons—to reduce their taxes or their personal liability risks. However, in both cases there are complications that you should be aware of.

Taxes

Although there's little difference in the tax liability between a sole proprietor, a general partnership, and an LLC, it's probably true that you can reduce your taxes if you form a corporation. However, there are many complications involved in taking advantage of this benefit (see chapter 17 for more information).

Liability

The issue of reducing risk by choosing a business entity is also very complicated (see chapter 17 for more information). A lawsuit can put your current assets, your savings, your retirement investments, and your future earnings at risk (see page 104). A sole proprietor is personally responsible for all the liability associated with her business. However, forming a general partnership doesn't reduce this risk—in fact, it exposes you to additional risks associated with your partner's actions. Forming a corporation or LLC can provide some limited liability, but it can never eliminate all the risks of running your business.

The Five Factors to Consider

There are advantages and disadvantages to each kind of business entity. Before you make a decision (other than a sole proprietorship), you should consider the cumulative impact of at least five factors—record-keeping complexity, business fees, control of the business, tax implications, and liability risks. These five factors are discussed fully in chapter 17, but here's a quick summary of their impact:

	Sole Prop	**Partnership**	**LLC**	**Corporation**
Record-keeping complexity	lower	higher	higher	highest
Fees	lower	higher	higher	highest
Control of the business	higher	lower	higher	lower
Taxes	higher	higher	higher	lower
Limited personal liability	higher	higher	lower	lower

Some of these five factors may be more important to you than others, depending on your circumstances. For more information about how to evaluate each of these considerations, see the more detailed explanation in chapter 17 and the "Considerations in Choosing a Business Entity" table on pages 189–90.

● ●

You Still Need to Be Fully Insured

No matter which business entity you choose, it's essential that you purchase adequate business liability, homeowners, and car insurance to protect your business and your family. Incorporation is no substitute for buying the proper insurance.

The cost of business liability insurance usually isn't affected by your business entity, but there may be some other differences:

- A partnership can list both partners as the named insured on one liability policy or list one partner as the named insured and the other as an additional insured. (You can also get two separate policies, but it will be more expensive.)
- If your business is a corporation, you won't be able to get a liability endorsement on your homeowners insurance policy; therefore, you will have to purchase a separate business liability insurance policy.

● ●

A Sole Proprietorship Is Usually Best

We believe that the best decision for the vast majority of providers will be to structure their business as a sole proprietorship. There are some special circumstances in which it may be more beneficial to form a general partnership, an LLC, or a corporation—but these choices will be the exception, not the rule.

The special circumstances that might make it worthwhile to select another business structure are as follows. If you can't answer yes to at least two of these six statements, we recommend that you simply choose a sole proprietorship. If you do answer yes to two or more of the statements, a sole proprietorship may still be the best choice for you—however, you will want to consider all the issues described in chapter 17 before you decide.

- Your business is consistently earning an annual net profit of $30,000 or more. (Your net profit is the bottom line on **Schedule C.**)
- You plan to stay in business for several more years.
- There is more than one owner of your business.
- You plan to hire employees who aren't members of your family.
- You are comfortable handling the technical aspects of a corporation (keeping separate business records, filing payroll tax forms, filing corporate tax returns, and so on) or are willing to hire a professional to do this work for you.
- You want to set up a corporation because of the prestige that you believe it will confer to your business, or for other personal reasons.

Can You Change Your Mind?

If you can't decide which entity is best for your business, you should start off as a sole proprietorship. If you want to make a change later, you can simply establish a partnership, LLC, or corporation. You can start and stop a sole proprietorship at any time, without any special paperwork.

However, if you start out as one of three other business entities, it will be more difficult to switch later. To shut down a partnership, LLC, or corporation, you will need to consult a lawyer and a tax professional to make sure that you comply with all the applicable state and federal laws.

• •

The Food Program

Any licensed child care program, regardless of its business entity, is entitled to participate in the Child and Adult Care Food Program and receive Tier II reimbursements. To receive the higher Tier I reimbursements, sole proprietors and LLCs must either serve low-income children, live in a low-income area, or qualify as a low-income family. In a partnership, each partner must meet the income eligibility guidelines. A partnership or corporation can also qualify for the Tier I rate. For more information about the Food Program, contact a sponsor in your area (see appendix B).

• •

Incorporating Your Association

Many providers are members of at least one family child care association. These associations range from small support groups to large statewide organizations, and most of them aren't incorporated. This has both advantages and disadvantages:

- The advantages of not incorporating are that the group can operate very informally, and it isn't required to keep legal documents or records. (An unincorporated association may still be required to file state or federal tax forms and to pay some income taxes.)

- The primary disadvantage of not incorporating is that there is less legal protection if someone tries to steal money from the organization or if a group of people try to take over the organization and its assets.

Your association can choose to become a nonprofit corporation by filing the appropriate state and federal tax forms. The advantage of this is that the association can formalize its rules by establishing bylaws that will ensure that its decisions will be made democratically and in support of its mission. These formalities can help to sustain the organization, especially if there is a large turnover of members. The disadvantages are that the association must follow its own rules, keep meeting minutes, hold elections, and keep other records.

Before you make a decision about whether to incorporate your association, we strongly recommend that you consult an attorney about the consequences of each option and see which one best fits the needs of your group. An attorney or tax professional can explain the specific rules in your state and whether the association is required to file tax forms. For help, contact the National Association for Family Child Care (see appendix B), which may be able to put you into contact with some family child care associations that have incorporated.

No matter what form your association takes, it should purchase general liability insurance to protect its officers and members from liability lawsuits (see page 92).

• •

Tax-Exempt Status

Unlike an individual child care provider, a nonprofit family child care association can be recognized by the IRS as a tax-exempt entity, usually a 501(c)(3). This will enable the association to avoid paying federal income tax on its income and to get financial support from foundations (grants) and individuals (tax-deductible donations). However, also bear in mind that there are limitations on how much lobbying a tax-exempt organization can do to influence state or federal legislation.

• •

CHAPTER SEVENTEEN

Business Structure Considerations

Chapter Summary
This chapter explains the five factors that you should consider in choosing a structure for your business.

As explained in chapter 16, a sole proprietorship is the best business structure for most family child care providers. However, if you aren't sure whether that option is best for you, this chapter will help you decide by describing the five considerations outlined on page 173—record-keeping complexity, fees, control of the business, taxes, and liability risks.

We have heard that some attorneys have been advising virtually every family child care provider to structure their business as a one-person LLC. These lawyers stress the tax and liability advantages of this step, but say little about the disadvantages. This chapter will give you enough information to question anyone who recommends a business entity to you without explaining the complexity of the decision or learning more about your specific situation.

Record-Keeping Complexity
The record-keeping considerations for each entity include the different requirements for setting up each type of business and the complexity of the records that you need to keep as you go along.

Sole Proprietorship
A sole proprietorship is the simplest kind of business entity to establish and maintain. Unless you take steps to create another kind of business entity, the IRS and your state will automatically treat you as a sole proprietor. There are no forms that you have to fill out to start a sole proprietorship, and in most cases you don't have to register your business with any government agency—you become a sole proprietor simply by opening your business.

Although sole proprietors aren't usually required to obtain a federal taxpayer identification number, we recommend that you do so in order to reduce the possibility of identify theft and to protect your privacy (see page 123).

Although many providers who operate as sole proprietors find the record-keeping require-ments to be extremely challenging, they are far less complex than the requirements for the other business entities. For detailed information about the record-keeping requirements for a sole proprietor, see the *Record-Keeping Guide* and the *Tax Workbook and Organizer*.

Partnership

Each state also has its own rules about forming partnerships. You must write a partnership agreement that spells out the rights and responsibilities of each partner, and then you must operate under these rules. Although your state may have specific requirements about what your partnership agreement must contain, most of them cover the following major areas:

- What is the name of the partnership?
- How will the profits and losses be allocated between the partners (50-50, 60-40)?
- Who will be responsible for record keeping?
- How will decisions be made, and what will happen if the partners can't agree?
- What will happen to the business if one of the partners dies or becomes disabled?
- How will the partnership assets be divided at the end of the partnership?
- How can the partnership agreement be amended?

The record-keeping requirements for a partnership include keeping your business and per-sonal records completely separate. A partnership must also keep records that identify each of its assets, and this can get very complicated. If the partners contribute any assets to the busi-ness (such as equipment, furniture, or toys), these assets are co-owned by both partners. Any items that the partnership purchases after it begins are the property of the business, and can't be owned by a partner. (The law in this area is very complex, and we recommend that you consult a tax professional.)

LLC

Setting up a one-person LLC is more involved than setting up a sole proprietorship. Although the state rules vary, in most cases you will be required to choose a business name and register it with the state, obtain federal and state taxpayer identification numbers, open a separate business bank account, and keep your business and personal records completely separate. If you want to establish a partnership or corporate LLC, your state may have addi-tional requirements, such as preparing an operating agreement.

Corporation

When you form a corporation, you must follow your state's requirements, which are usually like those for an LLC. In addition, most states require corporations to do the following:

- Identify its corporate officers and directors.
- Draft articles of incorporation.
- Apply for a state charter to operate.
- Adopt bylaws and issue stock to the owners.

- Hold a stockholder meeting and keep minutes, then continue to meet annually and keep regular minutes.
- Set up a federal and state payroll tax withholding program.
- Establish rules for what will happen if one of the owners becomes disabled or dies.
- Set up and maintain a precise balance sheet record of all income and expenses. (You may need an accountant to keep these records, and you may also be required to save the records longer than a sole proprietor.)

When you set up a corporation, you must be treated as an employee in order to draw a salary. This means that the business has to set you up as an employee and withhold federal —and possibly state—payroll taxes and file quarterly and annual employment tax forms. (A sole proprietor doesn't have to file these tax forms unless she hires an employee.)

••

Separate Records

If you form a partnership, LLC, or corporation, you will be required to keep your business and personal records completely separate, and this can be difficult. Many of the expenses in a family child care business—including furniture, appliances, home repairs, toilet paper, and cleaning and kitchen supplies—are used by both the business and the provider's family. This means that you will have to initially pay for these expenses out of your personal checking account, then calculate the business portion of your purchases and write a check from your business account to reimburse yourself. You will also need to save both the original receipt and the records of the reimbursement. It can be very tedious to keep all these detailed records for every purchase. (A corporation can use one of the accounting software programs designed for corporations, such as *Quickbooks*, *Mind Your Own Business*, or *Peachtree Accounting*.)

••

Business Fees

This section describes the differing fees that are required for each business entity, including filing fees, annual business fees, workers' compensation insurance, and tax preparation fees. Bear in mind that some states also have small licensing fees—usually less than $100—that are required for a new family child care business, regardless of the business entity.

Sole Proprietorship

- There are no state filing fees that you have to pay for establishing a sole proprietorship and no annual fees for maintaining the business.
- Sole proprietors aren't required to buy workers' compensation insurance unless they hire employees.

- If you pay someone to prepare your taxes, the tax preparation fees will be lower for a sole proprietorship than for a partnership or a corporation.

Partnership
- Although there are no federal fees to start a partnership, there may be state business license fees.
- A partnership usually isn't required to buy workers' compensation insurance unless it has nonpartner employees.
- The tax preparation fees for a partnership are higher than for a sole proprietorship because a separate return must be prepared for the partnership.

LLC
- When you establish an LLC, you must pay a state filing fee that usually ranges from $50 to $500. (For the fee in your state, see www.cst.net/paralegal/statefee.html.)
- An LLC may have to pay annual state business fees.
- An LLC probably won't have to buy workers' compensation insurance unless it hires an employee.
- The tax preparation fees for a one-person LLC should be about the same as a sole proprietor (lower).
- An LLC may find it easier to borrow money than a sole proprietor or partnership, but some lenders will still require you to personally guarantee the loan.
- In some states you may be required to file a notice in a local newspaper saying that your business has been formed.

Corporation
- When you establish a corporation, you must pay a state filing fee, and these fees vary widely by state. (For the fee in your state, contact your secretary of state's office.)
- A corporation may have to pay annual state business fees.
- A corporation will probably have to buy workers' compensation insurance.
- The tax preparation fees for a corporation will be higher since corporate tax forms have to be prepared, and they are quite complex.
- A corporation may find it easier to borrow money than a sole proprietor or partnership, but some lenders will still require you to personally guarantee the loan.
- In some states you may be required to file a notice in a local newspaper saying that your business has been formed.

• •

Workers' Compensation Insurance

Workers' compensation insurance covers injuries that are suffered by employees on the job (see pages 87 and 89). This insurance can cost thousands of dollars, and there are different state rules about when it's required. In some states sole proprietors and one-person LLCs aren't required to have it. In other states it isn't required for one- or two-person corporations who have no employees—or it may only be required if you have a certain number of employees. A partnership may not be required to buy it if all the employees are family members.

Ask your state department of labor about the workers' compensation insurance requirements in your state. If this insurance is required and you don't have it, the penalties can be very high—hundreds of dollars a day. You may also be responsible for all the medical costs associated with an employee's injury, including disability income payments.

• •

Control of the Business

Your "control of the business" is how much say you have in making the decisions in your business. You will have the most control over your business as a sole proprietor and the least control as a corporation.

Sole Proprietorship

If you are a sole proprietor, you have full control over all the decisions that affect your business. You have no partners or corporate directors to consult and must only abide by the minimum legal requirements (such as those for the ADA, price fixing, and discrimination) that apply to any business owner. You get to keep all of the income from the business and must cover all of the losses. If you want to close down the business, you simply stop working and don't have to file any special forms.

Partnership

In a partnership, the control of the business is divided between the partners. Although the division of responsibility can vary (based on the partnership agreement), no one partner can make all the decisions. If you are used to running your own business, you may find it more difficult to work with a partner. In fact, conflicts between partners are the most common reason that partnerships fail. Either partner can end a partnership at any time.

On the other hand, a partnership allows you to draw on the different—and ideally complementary—business skills of two people. Also, if you would like to work with another person, a partnership is a simpler form of business organization than a corporation.

LLC

A one-person LLC has total control over the business, just like a sole proprietor. In a partnership or corporate LLC, the control of the business is spread between the members, as described in the operating agreement. In a partnership LLC, the control of the business works in the same way as a partnership. In a corporate LLC, the final decisions rest with the board of directors, although you may have effective control over the board.

A one-person LLC ends whenever you stop doing business and is as easy to close as a sole proprietorship. It's more difficult to close a partnership LLC or a corporate LLC; most states require a waiting period before you can dissolve one of those entities (see page 186).

Corporation

In a corporation, the shareholders elect a board of directors that is ultimately responsible for all the important business decisions. In most states, there must be at least three people on the board. However, in some states you could set yourself up as the sole director, and in others you and your husband could be the only directors. But even if you find a way to maintain effective control over the business, you must still operate under the rules of the corporate bylaws and articles of incorporation, which may put some limits on what you can do.

Tax Implications

If we simply consider the issues of record keeping, fees, and control, we believe that a sole proprietorship is clearly the best business entity for most family child care providers. However, now we will add a consideration of the tax advantages and disadvantages of each business structure.

Sole Proprietorship and One-Person LLC

The federal tax rules are exactly the same for a sole proprietor and a one-person LLC. You will file all the same tax forms, claim all your business deductions the same way (including home expenses on **Form 8829**), and pay the same amount in taxes (Social Security and Medicare taxes as well as state and federal income taxes on the profit from your business).

Partnership

In a partnership, the business itself doesn't pay any income taxes, but the partners pay the same taxes as a sole proprietor. Each partner pays Social Security and Medicare taxes and state and federal income taxes on their share of the profit. This means that a partnership has no tax savings over a sole proprietorship.

However, as a partner you will file different tax forms than as a sole proprietor. The business itself will file partnership tax forms (**Form 1065 U.S. Return of Partnership Income**) and each partner will file their own tax forms, including **Form 1065 Schedule K-1 Partner's Share of Income, Credits, Deductions.** Another difference is that a partnership can't claim any home expenses (such as property tax, mortgage interest, utilities, repairs, home improvements, and home depreciation) as a business deduction on **Form 8829.**

Instead, it would have to pay rent to the homeowner and the homeowner would have to report this rent as income on **Schedule E.** The homeowner could then claim her home expenses as deductions. However, she wouldn't be able to deduct the same amount of home expenses on **Schedule E** as she could on **Form 8829** if she was a sole proprietor. The bottom line is that you lose some home deductions if you form a partnership.

Two Types of Corporations
In considering the tax implications of incorporating, we need to distinguish between two types of corporations, C corporations and S corporations:

- *C Corporations.* The advantage of a C corporation is that you can set up tax-free employee benefits (such as a pension plan, disability income insurance, and health insurance for you and your family) that reduce the amount of Social Security taxes that are owed. The disadvantage is that any corporate profits that aren't paid out as salaries are double-taxed—once as corporate profits, and again as individual income. When a C corporation pays out all its profits as wages, it offers no tax benefit over a sole proprietorship.

- *S Corporations.* The advantage of an S corporation is that the corporate profits are only taxed once, when they are paid as salaries or profits, since there is no corporate tax. In addition, if the business has a loss, you (as the owner) can deduct it on your personal tax return. (In a C corporation any losses must be offset against future corporate profits.) If your business is likely to have a loss, an S corporation is clearly the better option.

A C corporation is usually more advantageous if you have substantial profits, while an S corporation is usually better if your income is smaller. However, there are other factors to bear in mind if you are considering either of these two types of corporations, including the number of shareholders, the ability to raise money, stock offerings, and other topics that are too involved to discuss here. Consult a tax professional and an attorney before you make a decision. As a family child care provider, you will probably find that the option of an S corporation makes more sense, and so we will use this option in the rest of this discussion.

S Corporation
When you form an S corporation, the corporation will hire you as an employee and withhold federal and state payroll taxes. This will only save the corporation a very small amount in taxes (about $18 per $1,000 of wages paid). However, an S corporation will usually pay out part of the corporate profit in wages and distribute the rest to you (the owner) as corporate profit on which you will only owe income tax, not Social Security or Medicare taxes, and this is where you will see a definite tax savings.

On every $1,000 that is distributed as corporate profit, the corporation will save about $150 in taxes. If the corporation has a $20,000 profit and you get half as employee wages and half as corporate profit, the tax savings will be about $1,500. Since you have less earned income, it's possible that some of your income will be taxed at a lower tax bracket, or that you may become eligible for certain tax credits, such as the Earned Income Credit.

However, these tax benefits come at a price:

- The corporation will owe federal and perhaps state unemployment taxes, which range from about $10 to $38 per $1,000 of wages paid. (Since this tax is deductible, the net cost to you will be lower.) The other business entities don't have to pay this tax unless you hire employees.

- The corporation is required to file all the employer payroll tax forms—such as quarterly **Form 941, Form 940, W-2, W-3,** and any state payroll tax forms—even if you are the only employee.

- The corporation may have to pay state filing fees, annual business fees, and higher tax preparation and accounting fees.

- The corporation must file quarterly estimated federal and state income tax forms. If you aren't incorporated, you can probably avoid filing these forms if your spouse has enough money withheld from his paycheck. (A single provider will almost always be required to file quarterly estimated tax forms, regardless of her business entity.)

- An S corporation can't gain a tax advantage by distributing some of the corporate profit to the owner (you) as a tax-free employee benefit or retirement pension, thereby reducing your Social Security and Medicare taxes. The tax rules forbid S corporations from deducting employee benefits. In addition, since recent changes have increased the contributions that sole proprietors can make to their retirement plans, there's little to be gained by forming a corporation in this regard. (The only remaining advantage is that corporate tax returns are typically less likely to be audited than those of a sole proprietor.)

- Like a partnership, neither an S nor a C corporation can claim business deductions for home expenses on **Form 8829.** The corporation could pay you rent, which you would have to report as income, and then you could claim some house deductions on **Schedule E.** But after all this extra record keeping, the net result would be a loss of some tax deductions, as compared to a sole proprietor.

Because of the extra taxes and paperwork involved, tax professionals say that it doesn't make financial sense to incorporate unless your business profit (the "bottom line" on **Schedule C**) is consistently at least $30,000. But even if you meet this requirement, incorporation isn't necessarily the best choice; you should consider all five factors described in this chapter when making your decision.

Before considering the tax implications, we had concluded that a sole proprietorship would be the best option for almost all providers. When we add the tax issues, the picture becomes a bit more complicated. Basically, there are no tax advantages involved in forming a partnership or an LLC, and there are some advantages for incorporating. However, you should consider the extra costs and paperwork involved to see if the tax benefit will be worth it. Bear in mind that if you hire someone else to keep your payroll records and prepare your taxes, this will be an additional expense.

• •

About Hiring Employees

Regardless of your business entity, you can hire employees for your business, including family members, and the record keeping required for federal taxes will be the same. The only difference is that if you are a sole proprietor or a one-person LLC, you can hire your own child under age 18 and not have to pay any Social Security, Medicare, or federal unemployment taxes. (All other business entities have to pay these taxes, regardless of the child's age.) In addition, partnerships and corporations may have to pay state unemployment taxes, which would minimize the primary tax benefit of hiring your own children.

• •

Liability Risks

Limiting their personal liability is the primary reason why some providers consider establishing a business entity other than a sole proprietorship. However, like the tax issues discussed above, this issue is also complicated.

Sole Proprietorship

As a sole proprietor, you are personally exposed to all the risks associated with your business (as described throughout this book). If you're married, this personal exposure may also directly affect your spouse and children. The worst-case scenario is that a child in your care is seriously injured in an accident, and the child's parents sue you and win a judgment of hundreds of thousands of dollars. Although your state laws may allow you to keep your home and some other assets, your future income can be attached. If you later remarry, inherit from a will or trust, or get a job, you may be forced to turn over your income to pay the judgment.

You can reduce this financial risk by buying adequate business liability insurance, which can protect you from most liability risks. You should purchase as much of this insurance as you can afford and is available to you. (See chapter 8 for more information.)

Partnership

Forming a partnership doesn't limit your liability in a lawsuit. Your personal assets are at risk in the same way as a sole proprietor, and there is added risk to you from the actions of your partner. Both partners are bound by the actions of either one in regard to parent contracts, and both partners are personally liable for all of the partnership's liabilities. For example, if the partnership takes out a business loan and can't pay it back, or if the business bounces a check, both partners are personally liable for the entire debt.

Both partners need to buy business liability insurance to protect themselves against their business risks. If you are going to set up a partnership, it may be best to form an LLC partnership because of the added protection of limited liability. (Consult an attorney.)

In some states you can form a limited liability partnership, which usually consists of at least one general partner and one limited partner. The general partner retains control over the business and is responsible for all the debts and risks. The limited partner has limited liability but can't participate in making the business decisions. This will not be a good alternative for most family child care providers (see page 171). If you are considering it, consult an attorney who can advise you whether it would make sense in your situation.

LLC and Corporation

When you incorporate your business or establish an LLC, you establish a separate legal entity that limits your personal liability. This means that you are no longer personally liable for the debts of the business; in a lawsuit, only the business assets would be at risk. For example, let's say that you have $4,000 in business assets (toys, business equipment, and a business checking account). If you were successfully sued, only these assets could be attached. Your personal assets—home, retirement funds, car, boat, personal checking and savings accounts—would be safe.

However, incorporation won't protect your personal assets if you personally guarantee a business debt (which your bank may require) or commit negligence or other wrongful acts. In other words, if you negligently shake a baby or are found negligent in a SIDS death or guilty of child abuse, your personal assets would be at risk, even if you were incorporated.

Incorporating your business or forming an LLC can be a first line of defense against lawsuits. The fact that you are incorporated or have formed an LLC may serve to discourage someone from suing you because they believe that it will be more difficult to win against a corporate entity. However, if the corporation is sued despite this, you will need to pay for your legal defense, and you will need to have business liability insurance to cover this risk. Incorporation is never a substitute for buying adequate business liability insurance.

Incorporation can also leave you exposed to the following risks:

- If you rent or lease a vehicle (or other equipment) to the corporation, and it's involved in an accident, you could be held personally liable.

- You aren't shielded from liability if you're driving your own car and are involved in an accident while on corporate business.

- If a member of your family commits child abuse or negligently causes an injury to a child, that person doesn't have limited liability and can be sued personally.

- A corporation or a partnership or corporate LLC can be sued even after it has ceased doing business or the owner has died. To dissolve one of these entities, you have to wait for a time period specified in the state laws during which claims can still be made against your business.

- If you are personally sued for something that has nothing to do with your business (personal bankruptcy, you have a creditor, you injure someone at a party), your business assets would be vulnerable in any judgment.

Piercing the Corporate Veil

Even if you incorporate or form a one-person LLC, a court can still break down your liability protection under certain circumstances. This is called "piercing the corporate veil," and it may happen if you commit fraud, break the law, or don't treat the corporation as a distinct legal entity—in other words, if you ignore the special rules and formalities that a corporation must follow and treat the business as your personal tool.

This means that if you form a corporation or a one-person LLC, you need to abide by the following rules in order to maintain your limited liability protection:

- Compile a list of your business assets. If you have few business assets it will be easier for a court to rule that you aren't acting like a corporation. If you're using most of your business toys and equipment for both business and personal purposes, you may not have very many business assets. However, you need to make sure that there are some resources that are specifically identified as business assets. You can do this by transferring some of your personal assets to the business, by buying business equipment from a business account, or by depositing enough money in a business account to cover the foreseeable expenses and cash reserves.

  On your list, identify the items used in the business that are business assets paid for out of the business account. Also identify the items (such as a swing set, second television, or children's furniture) that you own and would like to transfer to the corporation. Prepare a list of these assets and draw up a formal document that transfers them to your business. (Bear in mind that transferring these assets may put them at risk in a lawsuit.)

- Buy business liability insurance. Business liability insurance can protect your assets in the event that your limited liability status is ignored by a court. It also protects you from lawsuits and claims against your business, and pays for your legal defense. Just because you are incorporated doesn't mean that someone can't sue you, and if this happens you will need insurance to pay your legal fees.

- Keep completely separate books, records, and bank accounts for your business. If you are incorporated, conduct regular shareholder and director meetings, record the minutes of these meetings, and follow your corporate bylaws.

- Identify your program as a corporation or LLC by listing your business name showing that you are a corporation or LLC on your advertisements, business cards and business checks, telephone listings, letterhead, envelopes, signs, and so on. When you sign anything related to your business (contract, policies, payment receipts, Food Program claim forms) always identify yourself as an LLC or an officer of the corporation.

- Keep your business and personal funds completely separate. If you combine your business and personal funds, you run the risk of losing your limited liability protection. This means that you can't pay any business expenses out of your personal checking account or write a check for a personal expense out of your business account.

Bear in mind that this list isn't comprehensive—the courts may find some other reason to "pierce the corporate veil." In addition, each state uses its own standards to determine when the corporate officers can be held personally liable.

Although it may be difficult to abide by these rules, failing to follow any one of them can expose you to personal liability even if you are a corporation or an LLC. To receive the protection of limited liability, you must not only set up your business properly, you must always treat it as a separate entity.

Special Liability Issues for LLCs

LLCs are a relatively new business entity that allow you to take advantage of the most favorable aspect of incorporation (limited liability) without all the complexity of that option. However, because LLCs are so new, there haven't been many lawsuits involving them in the state courts—and some courts that have a history of protecting corporations in liability lawsuits may be reluctant to offer the same protections to LLCs. In other words, some state courts may find it easier to "pierce the corporate veil" when a lawsuit arises that involves an LLC.

If you form a one-person LLC, you should be especially careful to follow all the formalities to maintain your limited liability protection. In particular, you should be careful about keeping separate records. Since a one-person LLC fills out the same tax forms as a sole proprietor, you may be tempted to become lax in keeping your business and personal funds completely separate from each other.

For example, a one-person LLC is entitled to depreciate her home and claim her home expenses on **Form 8829.** However, if you do so you could be identifying your home as a business asset that would be subject to attachment in a lawsuit. If the home is in your name, this may be enough to protect it from creditors if you are sued, but there isn't enough case law to be certain on this point.

If your business is a one-person LLC, and you sell your home, you can exclude your gain on the sale from taxes in the same way as a sole proprietor. However, if you are a two-person LLC, it will be much more difficult to avoid these taxes.

Which Business Structure Is Best for You?

You now have all the information you need to decide which business entity would be best for your business. Based on all the factors, a sole proprietorship will be the best choice for most family child care providers—the record keeping is simpler, the fees are lower, and the control is greater. Although incorporating can save you a little in taxes, it takes more work to get this benefit, and the other costs associated with incorporating may wipe out this advantage. And although an LLC or corporation can limit your personal liability risk, this isn't blanket protection, and you need to follow the formalities carefully to maintain it.

If you choose any option other than a sole proprietorship, we strongly recommend that you consult with an attorney and a tax professional to make sure that you understand all the implications of your decision and the state rules that apply in your case.

Considerations in Choosing a Business Entity

This page and the next provide a summary of the five factors that you should consider in making a decision about how to structure your business:

	Sole Prop	Partnership	LLC	Corporation
Summary				
Record-keeping complexity	lower	higher	higher	highest
Fees	lower	higher	higher	highest
Control of the business	higher	lower	higher	lower
Taxes	higher	higher	higher	lower
Limited personal liability	higher	higher	lower	lower
Record-Keeping Complexity				
Must register business with the state	maybe	maybe	Y	Y
Must register business name with the state	maybe	maybe	maybe	maybe
Must get federal tax ID number	N[1]	Y	N[1]	Y
Must get state tax ID number	N[1]	maybe	maybe	maybe
Must prepare an operating agreement or file articles of organization and bylaws	N	Y	Y	Y
Must open separate business bank account	N	Y	Y	Y
Must keep separate business and personal records	N	Y	Y	Y
Must file quarterly and annual federal and state payroll tax forms	N[1]	N[1]	N[1]	Y
Fees				
Must pay state filing fees	N	maybe	Y	Y
Must pay annual state business fees	N	maybe	maybe	maybe
Workers' compensation insurance required	N[2]	N[2]	N[2]	maybe
Tax preparation fees for the business return	lower	higher	lower	higher
Control of the Business				
Ability to control your business decisions	100%	shared	100%	board of directors

[1] Unless you hire an employee

[2] If you have employees you may have to buy this insurance. Rules vary by state.

	Sole Prop	Partnership	LLC	Corporation
Tax Issues				
Must file federal payroll tax forms (940, 941, W-2, W-3)	N[1]	N[1]	N[1]	Y
Must pay federal unemployment tax	N[1]	N[1]	N[1]	Y
Must pay state unemployment tax	N[1]	N[1]	N[1]	Y
Can qualify for Tier I on Food Program if your family is low income	Y	Y if both	Y	N
Can reduce Social Security/Medicare tax by distributing some of the profit as income rather than wages	N	N	N	Y
Frequency of IRS audits	low	low	low	lower
Save Social Security/Medicare tax and federal unemployment tax when hiring own children under age 18	Y	maybe	Y	N
Can deduct the business portion of car loan interest when using the standard mileage rate	Y	N	Y	N
Limited Personal Liability				
Limited liability for owner	N	N	Y	Y

[1] Unless you hire an employee

Conclusion

In this book we have tried to explain the business risks that family child care providers face and help you make informed decisions about how to manage them. We believe that understanding these risks is better than being ignorant of them. Our goal is to reduce the number of family child care providers who are surprised by—and therefore unprepared to deal with—a major financial disaster that could have been mitigated if they had taken preventative steps and bought the proper insurance.

However, after learning about all these potential risks, some providers just feel discouraged or depressed, thinking, "I could be sued for just about anything," "I can't possibly afford to buy all the insurance I need," "I just don't understand this, it's too much to comprehend," or even, "I'm thinking about quitting because I just can't cope with all this."

Managing business risks is a new way of thinking for many family child care providers, and it isn't a subject that you should expect to master overnight. We encourage you to ask your licensor or insurance agent about anything that you don't understand. If you do this, we believe that you can learn to make informed decisions and effectively protect yourself and your business.

Bear in mind that the risk that you will face a major lawsuit is extremely small, and that you can reduce this risk even further by following the business practices that are outlined in this book. If you follow those steps, you are less likely to be sued, any damages that are awarded against you are likely to be smaller, and your insurance policy is less likely to be discontinued.

Although it may not seem that it's possible to manage all of the risks described in this book, you can do it. In the end, don't lose sight of the fact that your business is about caring for children. It's for the children that you work so hard. We hope that this book will enable you to reduce your risks so that you can worry less and concentrate more on helping the children for a long time to come.

Appendix A
Sample Forms and Policies

General Field Trip Permission Form

As part of my educational program, I will take the children in my care on a variety of field trips away from my home. The typical destinations of these field trips include [add or subtract to suit your own program]:

    walk through the neighborhood

    walk/drive to the local park, public swimming pool, zoo, etc.

    walk/drive to local grocery store, school, local stores, etc.

Parents give their consent to such field trips by signing their name:

_____ (parent signature) _____ (date)

_____ (parent signature) _____ (date)

Specific Field Trip Permission Form

I, _____ (full name of parent), hereby give permission

for _____ (full name of provider) to take

_____ (full name of child) on a field trip

to the following location: _____ on ____/____/____

(month/day/year).

General Privacy Policy

I will do all that I can to protect your family's privacy and I will abide by our state's privacy law. In addition, I will keep all records and information about your child and your family private and confidential, unless I have your written permission to reveal specific information.

I ask that you also respect the privacy of my family by not sharing any information you learn about my family with others, without my written permission.

General Permission Form

My first priority is to protect your child's health and safety. To ensure that I am operating with your full understanding and agreement about your family's privacy, I ask that you grant me permission to conduct the following activities. Please initial each item for which you consent:

* Placement of photos of your child around my home _____
* Placement of photos of your child in photo albums for view by prospective clients and other families in my care _____
* Posting of artwork and other craft activities with your child's name on/in/around my home _____
* Occasional involvement of neighborhood children in indoor and outdoor activities with the children in my care _____
* Use of an electronic monitor to listen in on your child from another room _____
* Listing the name of your child or other members of your family in my client newsletter, and posting this information on my bulletin board _____
Other _____

Immunization Notice

All parents must inform the provider of all immunizations that their child has received. The provider is not able to inform parents about the immunization status of other children in the program. Therefore, parents who enroll in my program may come in contact with children who are underimmunized or not immunized. Exposure to such children may increase the risk of contracting disease.

Parents who choose not to immunize their child must inform the provider of their decision. Children who are not immunized run a higher risk of contracting a disease, transmitting it to others, and being quarantined if there is an outbreak.

Sample Pickup Policy

In operating my child care business, my first responsibility is to protect the health and safety of the children in my care. When parents drop off and pick up their children, I want to make sure that the children are being transported safely. When a parent transports children under the influence of alcohol or drugs or fails to use an appropriate car seat, it creates an unsafe situation for the children.

If, in my opinion, a child cannot be safely transported to or from my home, I will ask the parent not to transport the child and will propose the alternatives listed below.

If the parent refuses to agree to one of these alternatives and insists on transporting the child, I will immediately call the police and report the unsafe driving situation.

1) I will call someone to pick up the child from the following list of people who are authorized to do so:

   _____   _____
   Name   Phone number

   _____   _____
   Name   Phone number

   _____   _____
   Name   Phone number

2) I will call a cab to pick up the child and the parent. The parent will pay the cab fare.

3) If the parent has failed to bring an appropriate car seat for the child, I will ask the parent to drive home without the child and return with an appropriate car seat installed in the car. I ___ will / ___ will not charge a late pickup fee under these circumstances.

4) Other acceptable alternatives proposed by the parent:

   _____

   _____

Appendix B
Organizations and Resources

Organizations

ADA Information Line
U.S. Department of Justice
800-514-0301; 800-514-0383 TTY
This phone line provides information and answers questions about ADA requirements.

American Academy of Pediatrics
141 Northwest Point Boulevard
Elk Grove Village, IL 60007-1098
847-434-4000
www.aap.org
This site offers resources on parenting, first aid, child abuse, and child development, as well as the *Home Safety Checklist*.

American SIDS Institute
2480 Windy Hill Road, Suite 380
Marietta, GA 30067
800-232-SIDS; 770-612-1030
www.sids.org
This site offers information and resources for preventing SIDS.

The Arc
500 E. Border, Suite 300
Arlington, TX 76010
817-261-6003

www.thearc.org
This site provides information about mental retardation and developmental disabilities.
The publications that you can download here include *Child Care Settings and the Americans with Disabilities Act* (www.thearc.org/faqs/ccqa1.html).

Centers for Disease Control and Prevention
1600 Clifton Rd NE
Atlanta, GA 30333
800-342-2437
www.cdc.gov
Children's health information, including universal infection control measures for children who are HIV-positive.

Child Care Law Center
221 Pine St., 3rd Floor
San Francisco, CA 94104
415-394-7144
www.childcarelaw.org
This organization provides answers to legal questions and offers a range of publications about legal issues in child care, including the following:

- *A Child Care Advocacy Guide to Land Use Principles*
- *Child Care Custody Disputes: With Whom Can the Child Go Home?*
- *Legal Issues for Family Child Care Providers in California: Reporting Child Abuse*
- *Legal Issues for Family Child Care Providers in California: Employing an Assistant*
- *Caring for Children with Special Needs: The Americans with Disabilities Act (ADA) and Child Care*
- *Caring for Mildly Sick and Injured Children*
- *Questions and Answers about the Americans with Disabilities Act: A Quick Reference (Information for Child Care Providers)*
- *Caring for Children with HIV or AIDS in Child Care*
- *Why and How to Locate Legal Resources for Child Care*
- *How to Find and Use a Lawyer*

CJ Foundation for SIDS
Hackensack University Medical Center
30 Prospect Avenue
Hackensack, NJ 07601
888-8CJ-SIDS or 201-996-5111
www.cjsids.com
This site offers SIDS information and resources.

Council for Professional Recognition
2460 Sixteenth Street NW
Washington, DC 20009-3575
800-424-4310; 202-265-9090
www.cdacouncil.org
This nonprofit organization offers the Child Development Associate credential program.

Children's Foundation
725 Fifteenth Street NW, Suite 505
Washington, DC 20005-2109
202-347-3300
www.childrensfoundation.net
This site has links to resources, state licensing regulations, and publications.

Enterprise Child Care
80 Fifth Ave., 6th Floor
New York, NY 10011
212-262-9575
www.enterprisefoundation.org
Enterprise Child Care links child care providers to housing opportunities and resources. They publish "Landlord and Tenant Issues for Family Child Care: A Resource Manual for Providers" (2000).

National Association for Family Child Care (NAFCC)
5202 Pinemont Drive
Salt Lake City, UT 84123
801-269-9338
www.nafcc.org
This site provides information on the NAFCC quality standards, accreditation program, and family child care associations.

National Association of Child Care Resource and Referral Agencies (NACCRRA)
1319 F Street NW, Suite 810
Washington, DC 20004
202-393-5501
www.naccrra.org
This organization keeps a list of local child care resource and referral agencies and has an online library of resources to promote health and safety in child care.

National Institute of Child Health and Human Development

NICHD Information Resource Center (IRC)
SIDS Back to Sleep Campaign
P. O. Box 3006
Rockville, MD 20847
800-505-CRIB or 800-370-2943
www.nichd.nih.gov/sids/sids.cfm
This site provides SIDS prevention information.

National Resource Center for Health and Safety in Child Care

1784 Racine Drive
Bldg 401, Room 106
Aurora, CO 80045-0508
800-598-KIDS
nrc.uchsc.edu
You can download *Caring for Our Children: National Health and Safety Performance Standards Guidelines for Out-of-Home Child Care Programs* from this site. (These standard guidelines were developed by the American Public Health Association, the American Academy of Pediatrics, and the Maternal and Child Health Bureau of the U.S. Department of Health and Human Services.)

National SIDS/Infant Death Resource Center (NSIDRC)

2070 Chain Bridge Road, Suite 450
Vienna, VA 22182
866-866-7437; 703-821-8955
www.sidscenter.org
This organization provides information and referral services for SIDS.

Nolo Press

950 Parker Street
Berkeley, CA 94710-2524
800-728-3555
www.nolo.com
A publisher of do-it-yourself legal publications that you can order online, including

- *The Corporate Minutes Book: The Legal Guide to Taking Care of Corporate Business,* by Anthony Mancuso
- *Incorporate Your Business: A 50-State Legal Guide to Forming a Corporation,* by Anthony Mancuso
- *The Partnership Book,* by Denis Clifford and Ralph Warner
- *Form Your Own Limited Liability Company,* by Anthony Mancuso
- *Incorporator Pro,* by Anthony Mancuso

Redleaf National Institute
10 Yorkton Court
St. Paul, MN 55117
rni@redleafinsitute.org
www.redleafinstitute.org
Our comprehensive Web site includes directories of tax professionals and insurance companies, as well as much more.

Other Resources

Online

- Links to state agencies that administer the Child and Adult Care Food Program: www.fns.usda.gov/cnd/Care/CACFP/cacfphome.htm

- Links to state licensing regulations: nrc.uchsc.edu/STATES/states.htm

- Online resource for finding insurance: www.insure.com; www.ehealthinsurance.com; www.searchingforinsurance.com; www.allquotesinsurance.com; www.intelliquote.com

- Links to credit bureaus: Experian (www.experian.com); Equifax (www.equifax.com; 800-685-1111); and TransUnion (www.tuc.com; 800-888-4213). To receive your credit report from all three companies, go to CreditReport (www.creditreport.com).

Publications

- Koskie, B. *Dealing with Maltreatment Allegations in Child Care Settings*. Minneapolis: Greater Minneapolis Day Care Association, 1993.

- Hungelmann, Jack. *Insurance for Dummies*. New York: Hungry Minds, Inc., 2001.

- Tyson, Eric. *Personal Finance for Dummies*. New York: Hungry Minds, Inc., 1994.

- Kendrick, Abby Shapiro, Joanne Gravell, and Massachusetts Department of Public Health. *Family Child Care Health and Safety Video and Checklist*. St. Paul: Redleaf Press, 1991.

- Patterson, John C. *Child Protection: Guidebook for Child Care Providers*. Alexandria, Va.: National Center for Missing and Exploited Children and the National Committee for the Prevention of Child Abuse, 1991.

- Murray, Kathleen. "Child Care and Child Abuse." *Legal Issues for Child Care Providers*, 1985.

- Fuller, Karen. "What Providers Should Know About SIDS." *Redleaf Business Bulletin*, (Spring) 2001.

Index